Covenant Bible Studies

COVENANT BIBLE STUDIES

1 Corinthians
The Community Struggles

Marcos R. Inhauser

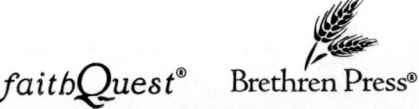

> *For a complete list of titles in the Covenant Bible Study Series, visit www.brethrenpress.com.*

1 Corinthians: The Community Struggles
Covenant Bible Studies Series

© 1994, 2016 *faithQuest*®. First edition 1994. Revised edition 2016. Published by Brethren Press®, 1451 Dundee Avenue, Elgin, IL 60120. For publishing information, visit www.brethrenpress.com.

FAITHQUEST and BRETHREN PRESS are registered in the U.S. Patent and Trademark Office by the Church of the Brethren, 1451 Dundee Avenue, Elgin, IL 60120.

All rights reserved. No portion of this book may be reproduced in any form or by any process or technique without the written consent of the publisher, except for brief quotations embodied in critical articles or reviews.

Unless otherwise noted, scripture quotations are from the New Revised Standard Version of the Bible, © 1989 National Council of the Churches of Christ in the United States of America. Used by permission. All rights reserved.

Library of Congress Cataloging-in-Publication Data

Names: Inhauser, Marcos R. (Marcos Roberto), author.
Title: 1 Corinthians : the community struggles / Marcos R. Inhauser.
Other titles: First Corinthians
Description: Revised edition. | Elgin, Illinois : FaithQuest, 2016. | Series: Covenant Bible studies series | Includes bibliographical references.
Identifiers: LCCN 2016034383 | ISBN 9780871782397
Subjects: LCSH: Bible. Corinthians, 1st—Textbooks. | Bible. Corinthians, 1st—Criticism, interpretation, etc.
Classification: LCC BS2675.55 .I54 2016 | DDC 227/.20071—dc23
LC record available at https://lccn.loc.gov/2016034383

20 19 18 17 16   3 4 5

Manufactured in the United States of America

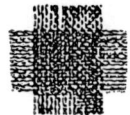

Contents

Foreword vii
Preface ix

1. **The Unity of the Body**
   1 Corinthians 1:1-17. 1
2. **The Wisdom of the Foolish**
   1 Corinthians 1:18–2:16 9
3. **Planters and Waterers**
   1 Corinthians 3:1–4:21 17
4. **In the Spirit of Gentleness**
   1 Corinthians 5:1–6:11 25
5. **The Freedom to Be Responsible**
   1 Corinthians 8:1-13 33
6. **All Things to All People**
   1 Corinthians 9:1–10:13 41
7. **Sharing Our Lives**
   1 Corinthians 11:17-34. 47
8. **Many Gifts, One Spirit**
   1 Corinthians 12:1-31; 14:1-40 55
9. **The Greatest of These Is Love**
   1 Corinthians 13:1-13 63
10. **Follow the Dream**
    1 Corinthians 15:1-58. 71

Resource Pages 77
Bibliography 85

Foreword

What does it mean to live a life of integrity and authenticity? What does the Bible say about the challenges we face at home, in the workplace, in our neighborhoods and communities? How does Christian faith inform the choices we make every day?

The Covenant Bible Studies series seeks to help participants find answers to these and other questions about living as faithful Christians in our world today. Each study encourages small groups to reflect, pray, and learn together.

Covenant Bible Studies are anchored in covenantal history. God covenanted with people in the Old Testament, established a new covenant in Jesus Christ, and through the presence of the Holy Spirit covenants with the church today. Thus, this Bible study is intended for small groups of people who can meet on a regular basis, gathering around God's word to discern its meaning for today, and share openly with one another.

An atmosphere of trust is built within the group, in which support will grow and faith will deepen. Each person's contribution is needed and valued. As each one contributes to study and prayer, the group becomes the real body of Christ. "For just as the body is one and has many members, and all the members of the body, though many, are one body, so it is with Christ" (1 Cor. 12:12).

Each chapter in this Covenant Bible Study is made up of four parts:

- *Prepare*—reading, studying, and reflecting on the material beforehand
- *Share and Pray*—fostering intimacy through personal sharing and prayer
- *Study*—exploring the Bible lesson together
- *Discuss and Act*—digging deeper into the biblical text, discovering its meaning for today, and preparing to go out again into the world

Welcome to this study. As you search the scriptures, may God's voice and guidance and the love and encouragement of brothers and sisters in Christ challenge you to live more fully the abundant life God promises.

Preface

Corinth, a prosperous seaport, was located at a strategic point between the Aegean and Adriatic seas. Daily, ships brought cargo and people from many other countries to this central location on east-west trade routes. The people who came to Corinth—Jews, Egyptians, Syrians, Italians, and Greeks—brought their own culture and religion.

There were no restrictions at the borders, not out of open-mindedness, but because people with merchandise kept trade and money moving. This was an ideal setting for the church, which also does not restrict who comes to it, but which must also deal with the problems of diversity and division.

This city operated by competition. Its life was characterized by individualism, ambition, and suspicion. People did not trust even their neighbors, everyone was considered a rival and competitor, and conflict was normal.

In both of Paul's letters to the church at Corinth, we see conflicts that were produced by these tensions in the larger society. Competing religious points of view were behind the discussion on meat sacrificed to idols (8:1-13) and wisdom as high knowledge (1:18-2:16). Different cultural conventions created discussion of the use of the veil by women in the church (11:1-6), women speaking in the church (14:34), and marriage and singleness (7:1-40). And business competition was the real cause for legal suits among church members, as Paul mentions (6:1-11).

There were two ways brothers and sisters in the church could avoid these tensions. They could adopt the individualistic practices of the larger society and ignore one another, or they could withdraw from the society to live a sectarian Christian life. The first solution destroys Christian community. The second one robs faith of cultural richness. Paul wrote his letters to the Corinthians to provide some guidelines for a third way. He points to a solution that includes Christian community and cultural diversity, believing that Corinthians could conform to Christian behavior and life while living in the society.

The problems Paul faced were not confined to the Corinthian church in the first century. We are now facing the same problems in our churches. Then and now, competition is the basis for many of our relationships. People are trained from childhood to excel, to earn good grades in school, to be better than others. Their worth is based on what they earn, not on who they are. Business is the daily bread. Every day people are fighting for better deals, for more profits, for cheaper prices. In addition, ethnic diversity is increasing in the United States. People from many other countries and cultures are living here. They bring their own practices, their foods, their languages, their religions with them. More and more, North American society is becoming a worldwide society, a universal culture.

What does it mean for the church today? What threats face our churches? What does it mean to be a Christian in a pluralistic society? Does the church have something to say and do in an individualistic, consumer society?

Scholars and students have approached 1 Corinthians from many angles. They have emphasized the gifts of the Spirit, the problem of earthly and heavenly wisdom, and Christian liberty. But from my point of view, Paul wrote to the Corinthians primarily to call for the unity of the body of Christ in an age of diversity. He spelled out criteria and principles for living in unity and for solving problems that threaten it. Everything he says about spiritual gifts, love, Holy Supper, Jesus Christ's body, maturity, and sanctification are his remedies for a divided church.

My prayer is for God's blessing and wisdom over us. My hope is that this Bible study not only will give us knowledge but will unite us as Christians to serve God.

Marcos R. Inhauser
Campinas, Brazil

1. The Unity of the Body
1 Corinthians 1:1-17

Prepare

1. Read 1 Corinthians 1. What surprises you about the way Paul begins his letter? What else do you notice about the format and content of this letter? Use a study Bible or other reference tool to see what was going on in the church at Corinth that prompted Paul to write to them.

2. Think of times you have experienced unity in the midst of diversity or differences. When were you able to agree to disagree? Were you able to move beyond tolerance to acceptance?

3. What makes a saint? Do you know any? Compare your understanding with the definition of saint in the session. How are you a saint in your life?

Share and Pray

1. Take time to get acquainted. Though some of you may have been in a group together in the past, remember this is a new time and you will become a group unique and special because of what each person

brings to this study. Take a few minutes to begin learning about each other.
    a. Give your name, where you were born, and where you began your faith journey (the church, its location, denomination).
    b. Tell briefly about the most exciting thing that has happened to you in the last year.
    c. Share one thing about yourself that the group is not likely to know.

2. Take time to begin forming your covenant group using the suggestions found in "Forming a Covenant Group," in the Resource Pages found at the back of this book.

3. Paul opens his letter with words of affirmation and thanks for the Corinthian Christians. Even though he later takes them to task for their divisions, stubbornness, and wrong understandings of some faith issues, he cares deeply for them. If Paul were writing to your church today, what would he list as his reasons to be thankful for the saints among you?

4. What are the areas of brokenness in your own life, your local church, and in your denomination?

5. Offer prayers of thanksgiving for the positive attributes of your church. With Paul, give thanks and affirm yourselves as God's beloved creation. Lift up the areas of division and brokenness in your own lives, your church, and your denomination. Offer prayers for healing and unity.

6. As your closing prayer, read aloud together Paul's salutation to the church in 1 Corinthians 1:1-9, making it personal by naming your own community in verse 2. For example, say: "To the church of God that is in Pittsburgh."

7. Sing or read "They'll Know We Are Christians by Our Love," or another hymn on unity in your hymnal.

In 1 Corinthians 1, Paul declares that the unity of the body of Christ (the church) has its foundation in the works of God. This affirmation is very meaningful when we consider that Paul is writing to Christians who could have been seduced easily by one of the many religious groups in Corinth. Paul affirms that Christianity is neither a human invention nor a human effort. People do not choose their faith from a menu. God chooses us and we respond. God and the works of God are the basis for the church.

> People do not choose their faith from a menu. God chooses us and we respond.

The Works of God

To what works of God does Paul refer? The first work, he points out, is that God has called them through Jesus Christ (vv. 1-17). God's calling is an exercise of sovereignty: God is able and has the power to call us, taking the first step to reach us. Our sins put us far from God, creating a gap between us and God, but God comes to us and calls us, as he did Eve and Adam in Eden. They had sinned, but God called them, providing garments for them. While we are still sinners, God calls us to be sanctified (v. 2) and to be incorporated (vv. 3-17) into the body of Christ.

A small church in Philadelphia ministers mainly to the poor and the homeless in the neighborhood, drawing people in, giving them help, and calling out their gifts. One man was a drug addict and an alcoholic, living in a refrigerator box. The church discovered him and accepted him into their fellowship. They assured him that God had need for his talents—assurance that gave him the strength and confidence to face his addictions. Now he is a lay leader, leading worship and music and fighting his destructive dependencies. God took the first step to save a man, despite his sins. God made him a saint in order that he might find new life.

Incorporated into the Body

At the same time we are taking on a new life, we are "incorporated" into the body of Christ. *Incorporated* is not a technical theological term. It is my word for what Paul means when he talks in verse 2 about the "church of God that is in Corinth." Paul is addressing the church, not individual Christians. Christians are called to be part of the church, to be part of the body of Jesus Christ. The salvation that God provides gives us forgiveness of sin, freedom from the slavery that sin produces (redemption), a declaration that we are now reconciled with God, new birth and life (regeneration), a new standard of life according to new values (sanctification), and incorporates us into the body of Christ, the church.

As the body of Christ, we are called to be in touch with God and also to be in touch with one another. Remember that from the beginning God said that it is not good for humans to be alone. People should be related to and identified with one another. The church is the place where we can be free from striving for individuality and self-sufficiency. God has called us to new life in the body of Christ. In my understanding of the gospel, it is impossible to be saved and not belong to the body of Christ, which is the church. There is no Christian alone. Without the fellowship of Christians there is no unified body to carry out Christ's mission. We deny Christ when we deny the centrality of the church, the *corpus Christi*.

> **In my understanding of the gospel, it is impossible to be saved and not belong to the body of Christ, which is the church. There is no Christian alone. Without the fellowship of Christians there is no unified body to carry out Christ's mission.**

When I was a pastor, irregular churchgoers would tell me that they could worship the Bible and pray alone, that they didn't need the congregation to be a Christian. Some said they could hear better sermons than mine in their own homes, sitting on their own comfortable sofas. Some of them said that all they see in the church is division. At least at home, alone, they are not affected by bickering. Have you heard this argument before?

We are bombarded by social forces promoting individualism. In schools, on television, on Facebook, in books, and in newspapers, we are pushed to be concerned first about ourselves. Every day we are pushed to be competitors. Some of us are convinced we can and should be Christians all by ourselves. We reason that no one else can do it for us.

Sanctified for Life in the Community

In some ways, sanctification does sound like a call to walk the lonesome valley all by ourselves. It means to set ourselves apart from the crowd and be devoted to a new life, even though the world lures us in a different direction. But sanctification does not lift us out of the world. It invites us away from rivalry and competition to a new community of believers who together become the body of Christ.

We get our word *saint* from the Latin word for sanctification. Through the life and death of Jesus Christ, God calls us saints not because we are perfect, but because God calls us to be Christlike. We are declared saints and we have to live as such. God doesn't save us just to remain in our sins and old lifestyles, but to live in newness of life. Corinth's Christians were called from immorality to morality, from discord to harmony, from division to unity, from self-centered individualism to community.

Paul is saying that the church has to be an organization that is made up of people who act differently from others in the society. Christians still live in the society but they no longer live by society's values. They are now Christians, and so they must live set apart with their Lord. They are dedicated to God and committed to new values of life. They are saints.

In the history of the church, people have tried many ways to be saints. Some have been completely obedient to scripture. Some have believed they could only answer God's calling by removing themselves from the world, so they created monasteries and devoted themselves to a life of rigorous prayer and meditation. Some have believed that God asks for self-denial and suffering, so they denied themselves many things and humbled themselves before God. But I believe that we cannot be sanctified for our own virtues. God offers us sanctification and we respond. God calls us to be in the communion of saints; we don't have to earn our way there.

The word *communion* comes from the conjunction of two words: *common* and *union*. Those who are incorporated into the body of Jesus Christ through salvation belong to God and to other members of the same body. We are not just members of the body as one is a member of a club or a political party; we are members of Jesus Christ's body by divine calling, through his works in our favor. All the body's members have in common the fact that we are united by the same salvation, sanctification, justification, and regeneration. We are "born again," new people with new lives.

As members of the body of Christ, we have to live in cooperation, because we are also brothers and sisters. The practice of calling each

> **We are not just members of the body as one is a member of a club or a political party; we are members of Jesus Christ's body by divine calling, through his works in our favor. All the body's members have in common the fact that we are united by the same salvation, sanctification, justification, and regeneration.**

other brother and sister in the church is an indication that this is more than an organization, it is the family of God. Addressing each other as family was particularly meaningful in history when the church was powerful and corrupt. Christians in those periods held unofficial and sometimes illegal worship in small groups modeled after the small, intimate, family-like churches of the New Testament. But even today, Christians long to belong together in church families where everyone is as close as a brother or sister.

To be in communion is to be united. We must be one because we have only one Savior and Lord, Jesus Christ, who is the head of this body. In the Corinthian church, it was common for people to be persuaded to follow this person or that person, believing that one was better than someone else. Some followed Apollos, some Cephas (Peter), others Paul.

Divide and Conquer?

Often when divisions appear in the church, it is the result of two or more groups claiming possession of the truth. Each group claims that they are faithful, illumined by God, and each group criticizes the others. Division is a way to claim superiority. Division is a way to praise people instead of praising Jesus. Division is a way to expend energy on something other than love. But in the body of Christ, there is no room for division because no one is superior to anyone else. All members of the body of Christ are members by the same calling and salvation.

> **Often when divisions appear in the church it is the result of two or more groups claiming possession of the truth. Each group claims that they are faithful, illumined by God, and each group criticizes the others. . . . But in the body of Christ, there is no room for division because no one is superior to anyone else.**

On my first day back from vacation at a church I served, an elder came to me and said: "Be prepared because there is a movement afoot to dismiss you." The next Sunday, the church board received a letter signed by thirty-one people asking for my resignation. Among them was an elder, a member of the church board. I asked for a meeting with the whole group to find out what was happening, what kind of criticisms they had, what they wanted, what I could change.

To my surprise, I discovered that they had spent two months in meetings, phone calls, and studies on my writings to discover "heresies."

They recorded my sermons to prove that I was preaching against church doctrine and visited church members to convince them of the charges. The fact that some people were against the pastor caused another group to support me and prove that I was faithful, preached well, and was grounded in denominational doctrine. It all sounded too much like the fight for leadership in the Corinthian church. In the end, we worked through it and I stayed. Churches that can face their divisions, keeping in mind their larger mission, are stronger. They are like a broken bone that becomes sturdier where it knits back together.

We are not Christians by ourselves, nor to ourselves. We have received from God all blessings through Jesus Christ and we must praise God for that. Since God does all things for us, we have no one to glorify except God. We glorify God when we live as saints in the new life in the body of Christ, set apart from the world by its goals but carried out in the world that God made and loves.

Discuss and Act

1. Look at the passage together. What problems did the church at Corinth face? How much like our own churches is the church at Corinth? Name the similarities. Who would be an Apollos, Cephas, or Paul today?

2. We talk a lot about Christian unity, but the church is full of dissension. What would it mean for the church to be truly united? Is the thought of real unity scary to you? Why, or why not?

3. In what way is your local church most united in spirit and thought? Share with one another the areas of common agreement on matters of faith, issues of the day, and church practices, such as baptism, music, communion, community action, and immigration.

4. Discuss whether division and disagreement play any useful role in the church. Distinguish between controversy that tears the church down and controversy that builds the church up. Which happens the most at church?

5. What does it mean to be united in the same mind? Can we be of one mind and have many different gifts and opinions? What is the overarching goal in your congregation to which all can agree?

6. Tell about some of the saints you thought of as you prepared for this session. Are they saints as Paul describes them? In what ways are you a saint?

7. How have you chosen to live a sanctified life, a life committed to working for Christ and the church? Is this a commitment you made for yourself alone, or are you working at the sanctified life as the church, the body of Christ? In what ways? In what way is your covenant group committed to a sanctified life? Consider planning to do one thing during this study that you feel called to do, using the talents of the group. For example, have Bible study with people confined to their homes; collect, sort, clean and mend clothes for a shelter or do repairs and cleaning; plan an outing with your church's youth and their friends.

2.
The Wisdom of the Foolish
1 Corinthians 1:18–2:16

Prepare

1. Read 1 Corinthians 1:18–2:16. Do Paul's words sound familiar? Recall other Bible passages that sound backward, such as the first being the last and the last being the first. Try applying this sort of logic in your life this week.

2. As you read this lesson, think of times God's wisdom has led you to do something foolish in the world's eyes. How did you feel? Would you do the same thing again? Why, or why not?

3. Who are the wise ones today? Name individuals or categories of people that the world considers wise. Make a list of the men and women whom you consider to be wise and some reasons why.

Share and Pray

1. Share a time when you made a fool of yourself. How did it feel to have others laugh at you? How did it feel to laugh at yourself? When have you done something that others thought was foolish but you thought was right?

2. Name some ways you would like to see the church become more "foolish." Name and celebrate ways your congregation has been "foolish" in the last few years.

3. Have each person in the group tell the story of their call to Christian faith—a moment when heart, soul, and mind found a home in Christ. If your group is large enough, share in pairs and then come back to the group and have each person tell a briefer version of their partner's experience.

4. In sentence prayers, give thanks for God's wisdom and foolishness. Invite each member of the group to ask for guidance and courage to be foolish for Christ in the church and in the world.

I remember the day someone said: "He is intelligent, but he is not wise." At the time, intelligence and wisdom meant the same to me. I used them synonymously. But I have since learned the difference between them. I discovered the difference in the Bible, which says that there is human wisdom, or intelligence, and the wisdom of God. The first is a product of human reasoning, the second is the knowledge we have, not from striving, but because God revealed it to us.

In the first session, we said that sanctification comes from God. Now we can add that wisdom also comes from God. Moreover, when we use God's logic and not our own, we are more tightly unified, because we are all using the same reasoning instead of our own various ways of thinking. From verse 18 through 31, Paul explains that God's wisdom is a fruit of God's sovereignty, but that does not mean that only God can exercise wisdom. We may also, but the wisdom we exercise must be God's wisdom and not our own.

God's Logic vs. Human Wisdom

Paul argues that God is so powerful that even when God is foolish, God is wiser than the wisest human, and God's weaknesses are stronger than the greatest human strength (1:25). How do we, humble people that we are, know what God's logic is? We look to Jesus Christ who is God's power and wisdom revealed to us in a weak and foolish way. The power of God's weakness is revealed in Jesus, who was a carpenter's son, born at the edge of the periphery. Israel was at the edge of the Roman Empire and Bethlehem was at the edge of Israel. God is disclosed in Jesus Christ, born into poverty, belonging to a powerless family, living without goods or wealth, dying crucified. Still, Jesus is the most powerful person in the world.

Everyone who intends to understand and to accept Jesus by human reasoning never quite understands him. Indeed, in several instances the Bible talks about Jesus Christ as a mystery that was hidden from human comprehension (see Eph. 3:5; Romans 16:25; Col. 1:26-27). The way that God elected to reveal divine wisdom seems crazy by human standards, an unreasonable way, contrary to all human wisdom.

Why would the almighty God wish to be incarnated and then die? Why did God choose to be poor? To be born in a manger? Why didn't God come in force with the angels to introduce the Son of God? Why did God come as one of the poor, befriend the poor, and speak to the poor? Because the poor, the uneducated, and the powerless have no access to earthly economic and political powers. They have only the power that God gives. They, more than the powerful, can depend on God because they have no worldly powers to hold on to. Christians, like the poor, are neither wise by human standards nor noble by birth (1:26), but they are both wise and noble when they live and think and operate with God's logic.

> **Everyone who intends to understand and to accept Jesus by human reasoning never quite understands him. Indeed, in several instances the Bible talks about Jesus Christ as a mystery that was hidden from human comprehension.**

Wise in God's Eyes

A mother and father and their children lived in a war-torn region of Central America. When the fighting came very near, the parents decided that it was time to move to the city where they would be out of danger. So they made their way with many other war refugees to the overcrowded city one hundred kilometers away. But they never felt at home away from the beautiful mountains and farms of the countryside. They were angry at the politicians and soldiers who had pushed them off the land.

Before they abandoned the farm, they had been studying the Bible in the nearby village. The priest was a long way away and only came to their town once or twice a year. In his place a lay leader, called a delegate of the Word, was appointed to lead the people in Bible study every week. The more they read and talked about the gospel, the more they understood their worth in God's eyes. The more they read, the more they realized they had power to live as God's children and strength to live out the scriptures.

With great daring, the family decided to go back to the farm. Amid criticism from extended family and friends who thought they were recklessly subjecting their children to unspeakable horrors, the family took their few possessions and went, unarmed, back to the farm. In spite of beatings, interrogations, harassment, the murder of a brother and a farmhand, the family remained on the land, strengthened by the wisdom of the gospel alone and the joy of knowing God's power.

Warnings against False Wisdom

This story illustrates the kind of wisdom Paul was promoting in Corinth. But first he had to critique the dangerous attitudes about wisdom that he found in the church and the culture around it. He warned them about wisdom that was based on special experience. In every age, not just Paul's, people claim to have special knowledge of the truth that others do not have. Their knowledge comes to them, so they say, by revelation, visions, and ecstatic experiences. This wisdom is at odds with our belief that God wants to be known by everyone, not by just a few with an inside track.

Paul also warns the church about wisdom that is based on scripture alone, as though scripture itself was divine. Philo, a Hellenistic Jew, was a leader of this movement. He used what was called the allegorical interpretation of scripture. Instead of reading the Old Testament as the record of God's people in history and how God acted in their favor, Philo supposed that nearly every text was an allegory, a highly symbolic story with hidden meaning. According to Philo, these mystical meanings were divine wisdom.

But Paul refused to elevate anything, including scripture, above God as the source of wisdom. In Latin America and North America, Christian apocalypticists come closest to treating scripture as divine. They search the book of Revelation and the prophets for hidden wisdom, giving the Bible equal or greater status than Jesus Christ.

Finally, Paul rejects wisdom based solely on intellect. He is critical of religious scholars who rely on sophisticated language, complex reasoning, and systematic logic to discover God's wisdom. They believe that wisdom is revealed through eloquence and persuasive preaching and teaching. Throughout Christian history, time and time again, brilliant theologians have tried to join human and divine wisdom. In our day, people are still persuaded by intelligence of this or that Bible scholar or theologian, as if God's truth can be discovered by study.

Paul rejects all these interpretations. The Holy Spirit's logic and wisdom, he says, are revealed to human beings in a strange and illogical way:

through the simplest language, spoken in weakness and fear. Paul knew that God doesn't need symbols or brilliance or experience to reveal the divine. God is so wise that God can impart divine wisdom using simple words, simple reasoning, using the weak in their weakness and the powerless in their fear.

Some Christians see God as triumphant, powerful, and supremely perfect, which is true, but God is only these things through suffering and defeat. God chooses to relate to an imperfect world, to take on flesh, and to suffer the same as we do. We are children of the God of heaven, who is also God on earth—with us in our successes and in our sorrows and pains. Our God can face all temptations that human beings face and suffer all the sorrows that human beings suffer and still be gracious and loving and perfect.

If salvation were decided by human reason, only well-educated, well-spoken people would be saved. If salvation were accomplished by human effort, only wealthy and powerful people would be saved. If salvation were determined by human virtue, churches would have to rank their members according to levels of education, wealth, and kindness. But even the brightest genius, the greatest millionaire, the most powerful leader, and the most generous person are less than the weakness of God. If our best is not good enough, no one could be saved. We are all equal in our unworthiness. In this way God puts all believers under the same condition in the body of Christ, without distinction by knowledge, birth, social status, or other human classification. In God's wisdom, everyone is worthy because no one is worthy!

Living through God's Wisdom

Paul urged us to use God's wisdom in the way we think and live. It is not a logic dictated by power, human intelligence, or richness, but rather a logic of the poor and powerless, a logic of pain and sorrows, a logic of victory through death. We are the people through whom God's wisdom is revealed in our simple speech and in our acknowledged weakness.

In 1990, I was part of an international delegation evaluating the economic situation in Peru and various projects financed by ecumenical organizations and churches. The government had just delivered an economic shock. Prices increased an average of six hundred percent, and food was scarce because of a long dry season. The unemployment rate was very high. We visited organizations working on development and churches involved with social programs.

One morning we went to a woman's house where eighty people were eating every day. I was expecting a big house, but the house was a poor one. When I asked the woman why she offered her house as a kitchen for eighty people, she said: "We are brothers and sisters. We must support one another in these troubled times. If each one of us tries to survive alone, what need is there for a church? The church is not just for good times; it is for bad times. We are not brothers and sisters just in good times; we are brothers and sisters in bad times too. This is the way we stay together as a body."

To offer your last possession when you don't have enough to eat is crazy, but the woman who gave her house so the poor could eat was wise.

Discuss and Act

1. Review the text. What do we do to get spiritual wisdom? Or do we simply receive it? If God reveals wisdom to us, why do some people seem to see it and others do not?

2. Paul reverses our understanding of wisdom and foolishness. We are called to be fools for Christ, to be faithful to Christ's claim on our lives even when the world thinks we are crazy. Can you think of a time you have seen someone be foolish for their faith? Describe the experience and talk about the positive results of this foolishness.

3. How have you been foolish for Christ? Who, if anybody, supports your foolish ways? How can the people in your covenant group encourage others to be foolish for Christ?

4. Compare the wisdom of God to the wisdom of a child. How does a child talk about God and reveal who God is? What have you learned about God and wisdom from children?

5. What does divine wisdom tell us about unity in the church? Is it foolish or wise, in God's way of thinking, to accept everybody in the body of Christ?

6. People search for wisdom several ways: through sage people who claim to communicate with the divine, through the scriptures alone, and by reason. Which of these do we rely on in our times? Would we be willing to give these up for God's wisdom? Do these ways of knowing have any value for us as Christians?

7. Return to the ideas for action you discussed at the end of session 1. In what way is sanctification foolish? How do you think others will perceive your action? Will they think it is foolish in worldly terms? Covenant together that your action will take some risk of being foolish to the world.

3.
Planters and Waterers
1 Corinthians 3:1–4:21

Prepare

1. Read 1 Corinthians 3:1–4:21. Paul uses many examples to illustrate his point. In the case of the parent, the farmer, and the builder, consider how each must cooperate as well as lead.

2. We say that we live "for the glory of God and my neighbor's good." But how easy is it to live this out in our society, which, like Corinthian society, is based on individualism and competition?

3. Who are the saints of your local church who have been the planters and the waterers? Often there are stories and legends of these saints. Think about what they have contributed.

Share and Pray

1. Look at your life through the lens of a growing tree, bush, or flower. Using paper and colored pens or crayons, draw an outline of this plant, including roots, a trunk or stem, branches or blossoms. At the root level, who are the people and what are the experiences that grounded your faith as a child? At the trunk or stem level, what

people and experiences have given strength to your growing adult faith and person? At the branching out or blossoming level, what experiences or people have contributed to setting you on a very different path of understanding?

2. What is planted in you at this time that is ready to grow? What is planted but struggling to sprout? What watering and tending do you need for this new life to grow? What is planted in your local church that is ready for growth?

3. Read this litany together:
   Leader: Watch! Wait! The day of God is at hand!
   People: Like the bud on a tree, God's possibilities are about to blossom!
   Leader: Stay awake! The reign of God is very near.
   People: We are here, watching and waiting with hope.
   All: May God bring justice to all people on this day.
   May God's reign come on earth as in heaven.

   Reprinted with permission of the publisher from *Flames of the Spirit*, ed. Ruth C. Duck, copyright © 1985 The Pilgrim Press, Cleveland, Ohio.

4. Come to God in prayer. Invite each person who chooses to do so to say out loud the name of one of the "planters and nurturers" mentioned in the first sharing exercise this week and offer a brief sentence about what he or she has done. The group responds: "For the gift of [name], God, we give you thanks."

5. Read or sing the hymn "There's a Church within Us, O Lord" by Kent Schneider. It's found online and in some hymnals. Listen carefully to the words as you read or sing them.

I **was in a small rural town in Honduras to hear about the people's lives and to learn about the community.** A mother of four spoke up saying, "I want to know which church has supported the woman who is working here with us. Before she came, our community was a battlefield where people were fighting against people, where jealousy and suspicion raged. Thanks to her ministry among us, we have learned that we were destroying one another. We learned that we must instead live in community, helping one another. We are now working together in a cooperative way, building up our community. I feel that our community is not formed only by the people who live here. When you sent this woman to work with us, I finally understood that we belong to a wider community and I want to know them."

This is exactly how Paul views the church—as a community. Throughout his writings he pictures the church as a body with many parts working together to make a whole. In 1 Corinthians 3 he adds the images of many builders working together to construct a building and the many people who cooperate to grow crops. In chapter 4, Paul makes a case for his own authority in the building up of the church. Corinthians are to think of him as their spiritual father and imitate him.

Strength and Cooperation

We like Paul's idea of cooperation, and we also know the value of strong leaders who can give direction to uncooperative groups. Which should it be? How do we balance cooperation with the strong leadership of key people in the church? How do parents balance authority with nurture in a family? How do citizens balance the value of every person with the need for strong leaders in a democracy? We clearly face many of the same struggles that Paul and the Corinthians faced.

Paul writes that unity is the result of cooperation (3:1-9), a willingness to work together to form a team. Cooperation produces a harmonious life (vv. 1-4) that is free from jealousy, quarrels, and divisions, while envy is the chief destroyer of cooperation and the main promoter of quarrels. Envy is a syndrome of "I want what others have" or "I want to be what others are." Jealous people envy power and public recognition; they want to be the chief, the leader of the community. They are in constant conflict.

While jealousy is the impulse to be like others or to have what they have, cooperation depends on having many differences but making them work together. In our society we are often driven by the need to be like others, to fit in. We want the latest fashions. We want to conform to certain social standards. We are embarrassed by odd or different people.

> **We like Paul's idea of cooperation, and we also know the value of strong leaders who can give direction to uncooperative groups. Which should it be? How do we balance cooperation with the strong leadership of key people in the church?**

But a society actually thrives on variety. In everything from gene pools to church boards, we need people whose various talents provide all that we need in life. We are well aware of the genetic effects of inbreeding, as well as the disastrous effects in churches where everyone wants to be the pastor!

Paul's familiar theme is the need for Christians to work in harmony and coordination. He uses the image of farming in chapter 3 to emphasize that just as no one person can farm alone, no one person can make a church. It takes the strengths and talents of many. "I planted, Apollos watered, but God gave the growth" (3:6). When a community works in a coordinated way, the ministries of each one are recognized, the objectives of the ministry are set (v. 7), and the results are the standard by which the community will be judged (v. 8).

A Common Purpose

A community recognizes the gifts and abilities of its members and uses all of them to build itself up. These gifts and abilities must be directed to reach the objectives that the community has. If each one uses his or her own gifts to achieve personal objectives, the community is not strengthened. So each one must be judged according to his or her willingness to work with the others toward the goal that God has set. There is no place for "stars," people who work only when they are spotlighted.

Paul also uses the image of building to illustrate the need for cooperation in Corinth, a commercial town more used to competition than cooperation. Forming the body of Christ is like building a building. Instead of a goal, like the harvest in the previous analogy, God provides us with the beginning point, the foundation on which to build—Jesus Christ. Paul claims to be the master builder who gets the project going. Others will build on his work. In a veiled way, Paul is talking about building up the temple of Christ. We are Christ's temple. Purifying fire will reveal whether the building is sturdy or whether it is weak. The builders will be spared, but their work together to form the temple (the Christian community) will be judged.

The strong building made of stone will survive, but the weak one made of straw will perish. The community has to pool its gifts, work together like master builders, and build the temple of Jesus Christ into a solid structure. Paul had worked at Corinth to break ground and establish the church. When he felt that the congregation had good skills and leadership to build and nurture the church, he left them for other points to preach the gospel and establish more churches.

Later, Paul got word about problems brewing in the Corinthian church, especially the divisions caused by members lining up in factions behind different church leaders. Some scholars believe that the main controversy arose around Paul's apostolic credentials and, consequently, his authority.

Leader vs. Leader

Technically, an apostle was one who had met and known Jesus personally. Corinthians argued that Paul never met Jesus Christ, his theology was very different from theirs, and he preached freedom from the law, which meant for them renouncing Old Testament laws that they had trusted for generations. Others believed that Apollos was more eloquent and persuasive than Paul. Apollos probably taught some variation of Christian doctrine, especially related to spiritual gifts. And some people began to judge Paul and his theology, saying that he was not wise because he had no spiritual gifts or had not taught about them. Surely a wise man would have firsthand communication with God and be holier than the usual churchgoer.

Some scholars believe that there were Christians in Corinth who, based on Paul's teaching about freedom, got involved with syncretism, that is, they tried to blend Christianity with other religions. If they were free from the law, they reasoned, it wouldn't hurt to indulge in some cultish practices. After all, lesser gods were no threat to Jesus. And so they ate food sacrificed to idols and raised controversy about women's ministry or marriage.

For me it is clear that there was a problem with Paul and Apollos. In the beginning of the letter, Paul mentioned Cephas' group, but now he points only to Apollos. People were judging between Paul and Apollos, each taking a side to criticize the other. Paul was under judgment. His claim to be an apostle was questioned, his theology was criticized, and his work was refuted. Envy and quarrels engulfed the church. Did Paul preach unity simply to quell the criticism of his ministry and restore himself as the chief leader, or was there actually room for both Paul and Apollos in the church?

Many churches in Latin America struggled with the same tension between authority and cooperative leadership. In response, they developed a way to be more democratic, especially where the church and dictatorial governments excluded them from decision making and power. Ordinary Christians started meeting in groups, believing that authority is given to those who serve others, who live as an example, and who have deep faith. Authority is not acquired from governments, but from God. Earthly authorities are mere caretakers of God's authority. God's deputies have to walk the edge of the razor that divides authoritarianism from cooperation.

Paul is walking that edge. When Paul wrote this letter, he had a strong feeling that the unity of the body of Christ was in danger. He always maintained that all authority rests with God ("God gave growth"). We are merely the field hands and the hod carriers, the "servants of Christ and stewards of God's mysteries" (4:1). A unified church has both leadership and cooperation under the guiding hand of God. Paul's intention was to point out some obstacles to this unity.

Obstacles to Unity

The first obstacle he lists is personal judgment (4:1-7). Human beings have a tendency to judge others, label, criticize, and order people around. But personal judgments have no basis in faith. They mean nothing, for only God can judge. That said, judgments still pull the community apart because we mistakenly put stock in them.

It is easy to judge another person using our own parameters, to compare someone against our own feelings and purposes (vv. 1-5). With false confidence we say, "If I were in your place, I would do better." From our imperfect vantage point, it is easy to judge wrongly and commit an injustice, to wrongly accuse as the Corinthians are doing to Paul.

Moreover, personal judgments classify people, labeling them as bad or good (vv. 6-7). Our judgments put "good" people in my group and "bad" people in other groups. This process of promoting oneself as one of the good is a process of humiliation of others (vv. 8-9). This is the double nature of personal judgment: In order to promote ourselves, we often have to humiliate our neighbors.

In the body of Christ, everyone has received all blessings from God through Jesus Christ. God reaches each one in his or her weakness, foolishness, powerlessness. No one has more or less than another; no one is superior or inferior to others.

After this, it is quite easy to understand why unity is broken when a community has judges and not brothers and sisters. The basis for unity is equality of members. In the body of Christ, everyone has received all blessings from God through Jesus Christ. God reaches each one in his or her weakness, foolishness, powerlessness. In the body of Christ, no one has more or less than another; no one is superior or inferior to others.

That town we visited in Honduras is a model of the balance between authority and community. An outsider joins the community as both a member and a leader. Her goal—and the community's goal—is to serve God and be a steward of God's authority. She was able to magnify the talents of the community by making them work together for God. Like Paul, her share in the community is leadership, not to garner power for herself, but to glorify God.

Discuss and Act

1. Take turns reading the text, having each person read a paragraph. List the different analogies Paul uses to illustrate his points.

2. Tell the stories of some saints of your congregation. Give thanks for the seeds they've sown, the way they tended the plants, and for the way God empowers the seeds to grow.

3. Paul connects spiritual immaturity with divisions and arguing in the church. What makes a Christian mature? Do you see less division among mature Christians? If you see as much or more division, is it positive or negative? Do mature Christians know how to handle conflict productively?

4. What does 1 Corinthians 3:11 mean when it says, "No one can lay any foundation other than . . . Jesus Christ"? What about leaders in your church? Can they guide the congregation? What about people with certain gifts?

5. Can a person be a leader sometimes and a follower at others? How difficult is that for you? Who in your church has final authority? When is that person a servant of the congregation?

6. Paul describes the people of Corinth—and us—as servants of Christ and stewards of God's mysteries. What do you think this demands of you as a Christian? What are God's mysteries?

7. Do you think Paul overuses his authority? His foes say he never saw Jesus and he has no gifts, yet he speaks with great authority. What are

the signs that Paul is truly a servant of Jesus Christ and not a boastful imitator of Christ?

8. How can leaders be encouraged to let others take the lead occasionally? And how can quiet or shy people be encouraged to take the lead once in a while?

9. Jesus Christ is our final authority. When people take too much authority and begin to judge others, they destroy the unity of the church. Tell of a personal experience in which judging destroyed a community or relationship. How are judgment and unity incompatible? Should we be disciplining each other in the church? How can it be done without judging?

4.
In the Spirit of Gentleness
1 Corinthians 5:1–6:11

Prepare

1. Read I Corinthians 5:1–6:11. As you read, think about ways that we discipline people in the church. Think of times you have seen church discipline used to punish people. Think of times you have seen it used to help people.
2. What is the difference between personal judgment and letting the church as a whole judge its members?
3. Have you ever been lovingly confronted by someone? Have you ever lovingly confronted another person? What was easy about confronting? What was hard about it? What does it feel like to be confronted by someone?
4. Paul counsels us to avoid judging people outside the church. We can only be responsible, he says, for the people in our church communities. How easy is it to separate ourselves as church people from ourselves as citizens in our society?

Share and Pray

1. Paul gives many examples of sins. This list is not exhaustive. What situations, experiences, or behaviors would you add to the list of ways that our human behavior reflects badly on the church and hurts the cause of Christ in the world?
2. What breaks the church down? What should we do about it as a church?
3. Some sins are personal; some are corporate; some have global ramifications. What are the sins of the church universal, our denomination, and our local church?
4. In a time of quiet confession, name the ways we are not faithful to God as the body of Christ in the world. Pray for God's forgiveness and healing and guidance.
5. Sing or recite together the words of "There Is a Balm in Gilead" or "O Healing River," found online or in many hymnals.

Immorality was rampant in Corinth. People came from all over the known world to live there, each with his or her own culture and morality. They had no roots in that city and no natural commitment to others living there. Many left their families, their communities, and livelihoods to make their way in a new place. Perhaps they felt free to do anything they pleased. There was no one to police their behavior because they were alone.

Cities of the ancient world were often centers of immorality and iniquity. In Genesis, cities such as Sodom and Gomorrah were considered degenerate places. Corinth was no exception. The church had to fight the allure of a city that teemed with "fornicators, idolaters, adulterers, male prostitutes, sodomites, thieves, the greedy, drunkards, revilers, robbers" (6:9-10). Paul urged the church to set itself apart under the discipline of the Christian community and to be, as it were, more like the City of God, the New Jerusalem.

"What would you do if you were a pastor in a church whose members were thieves?" a Chilean pastor asked me when I visited his church. His church is in a carboniferous area where several coal industries were closed by the economic recession. More than seventy percent of the people were unemployed. One method of survival was to rob coal from trucks, carry it to the seaport, and sell it. Is some immorality justified? What does the morality of the church require?

A Disciplining Community

In 1 Corinthians 5 and 6, we find a strong exhortation to be sanctified, that is, to live a holy life. We also get some criteria for life in the body of Jesus Christ. Paul tells the church that members of the body of Jesus Christ have to live in sanctification, and that members who sin must be judged by the religious community.

In our last study, Paul cautioned us about judgment, suggesting that we leave such decisions to God. Now he is asking the community to judge. The difference is that our personal judgments measure others according to our individual criteria and standards; we decide guilt or innocence based on what we would do, not on what is best for the person under judgment.

When each person is a judge, there are as many criteria as there are judges, and with so many judges there is no objective standard by which to make impartial decisions. Here, Paul asks the community to judge itself or its members against the morality prescribed by the full community, bringing everyone to the same standard and unifying the church.

> **Paul asks the community to judge itself or its members against the morality prescribed by the full community, bringing everyone to the same standard and unifying the church.**

Many of us harbor feelings of retribution. We want to punish someone who has done wrong, or we want to see them punished. But the church is called to judge not for retribution, but to bring a wayward member in line with a standard. Discipline is a way to walk with someone, to help people live in a better way.

A woman brought a story to the church board about how the pastor of the congregation made romantic advances toward her in a counseling session. As a troubled wife who was seeking advice for her crumbling marriage, she was vulnerable to the pastor's compliments and invitation to be friendly. After five or six sessions, they started an affair that lasted six months.

Though she was sorry she let herself be seduced, the woman argued that she should have been able to trust the pastor. He had a degree in counseling and was a minister, the supposed keeper of morality. He had encouraged her to become romantically involved with him as therapy, as a way to raise her self-esteem. What should the church board do? How will they help these people walk in a better way?

The Church vs. the World

Paul believes judgment is to be used to heal and restore the church. It cannot be used to demand that the world, which does not profess the community's convictions, come into line with the church. God will judge the world in the end. We can only keep track of the church. Therefore, Paul says, do not get involved in the civil suits and civil courts. To this day, some churches do not press suits or take their problems into civil courts.

The entwining of church and society in our age makes this separation difficult. Paul was more able than we are to call the church to a set-apart life, leaving civil matters to magistrates. Should we be more willing to conform to civil laws, for instance, when the government professes to be Christian? Should we allow congregants to sue pastors in court? Perhaps we are to take note of the subtle merger of church and state that this represents and examine our faith to see where our true loyalties lie.

> **Immorality is not simply an individual's problem that can be remedied by punishment. It has consequences for the whole community. When one member is sick, the whole church body suffers.**

Immorality is not simply an individual's problem that can be remedied by punishment. It has consequences for the whole community. When one member is sick, the whole church body suffers. This is the reason Paul emphasizes the necessity to discipline, not punish, those who live in immorality. He advises the church in Corinth to let the saints judge fellow saints and work out the discipline to restore the community.

Discipline is about keeping out the sin (not the sinner); it is also about promoting full life in the body. The body of Christ disciplines itself to live a Christlike life and must continually monitor its health. Just as we discipline ourselves on diets, in exercise, in patience, and in devotion, the church disciplines itself for the sanctified life.

Not All Sin Is Personal

When we talk about sin, we usually think of personal and individual sin. This is the way that doctrine has taught us. This is not the only dimension of sin, however. Sin also has a social dimension, that is, we can sin as a group as well as individuals. Just as someone else's sin can affect another, corporate sin may have a corporate victim, such as the church.

When people in Latin America and developing countries receive no more than sixty dollars a month for their jobs, they are not sinners because they can't eat enough to survive. When parents can't afford education for their children, they are not sinners. Society is the sinner. This is what liberation theology calls "social sin." People suffer the consequences of a sinful social structure.

In the same way, there are "national sins." We need to remember that on the day of the Lord, whole nations will be judged because of the injustices they have visited on other nations. For instance, wealthy nations have survived often not by their own merits, but by exploiting others. This is a national sin. Many wealthy societies are built on the blood, sweat, and tears of slave labor. For instance, when South Africa's whites reaped great wealth from diamonds that were mined by poor blacks, that was a national sin. When the United States supported a dictatorship in El Salvador at the expense of human rights and human lives, that was a national sin.

Sins on all levels affect the unity of the body of Christ. Personal sins destroy the communion with God and neighbors. Social sin divides people into rich and poor, educated and illiterate, black and white. National sins divide nations into developed and undeveloped—a standard which is often based on Western economic and industrial ideals.

> **Sin on all levels affects the unity of the body of Christ. Personal sins destroy the communion with God and neighbors. Social sin divides people into rich and poor, educated and illiterate, black and white. National sins divide nations into developed and undeveloped—a standard which is often based on Western economic and industrial ideals.**

Wisdom as God Defines It

The discipline of sanctification brings us back once again to God's wisdom, the wisdom that appears foolish to the world. In our litigious society where everyone is suing everyone else, we think it is foolish to reject the protection of the courts. It is bad judgment to forgive the person who destroyed your car in an accident. You must sue the person's insurance company. Spouses are suing each other, parents sue teachers, patients sue doctors, and children sue parents. But the world's wisdom is like the cost of medical care that rises to cover malpractice until fewer and fewer people can afford treatment at all.

Paul doesn't prohibit using the systems of the world as much as he promotes the logic of God's world. And in God's world it is sanctification that brings reconciliation. Instead of putting saints out of the fold for revenge, the body of Christ brings the wayward saint back in not to judge or discipline in private, but to encourage and guide the offender back into the community.

The parishioner who stole some bread to eat cannot be made moral by going to jail. He or she needs the community that looks after people's needs. The pastor who sexually abuses a parishioner cannot be made moral by handing over money for damages. He or she needs the guidance of a community that cares about each member and the health of the whole body. If the church is guilty of any corporate sin, it is the sin of failing to practice the difficult art of discipline.

Paul might just as well have been talking to the church today when he wrote to the church at Corinth. The issues have not changed much, nor has the truth of Paul's advice, which we would do well to heed.

Discuss and Act

1. In the last session, Paul discouraged judging. In this session, he tells us under what circumstances we may judge others. When should we judge people? What are the standards against which we should judge people? When is it appropriate to confront?

2. Paul approves of discipline and judgment that helps repair the community. How can we discipline for healing? How can we avoid the danger of disciplining for revenge or punishment?

3. In the past, congregations were often reluctant to reach out to the denomination or civil authorities in situations involving pastors, counselors, and youth leaders. Unfortunately, this allowed abusive behavior to go unchecked and people to be victimized. Where is the line between behavior that can be disciplined within the church and behavior requiring outside intervention? If your church has a policy for such situations, review it. If it does not, advocate for putting one in place.

4. Which sins are the most serious? Are some sins unavoidable, such as when the poor steal? What about sins of omission? What about corporate sin?

5. Paul says that we should only discipline people in the church; we cannot be responsible for people who have not chosen the standard of Jesus Christ. Is it possible today to clearly distinguish church people from non-church people? What should we do in cases where Christianity conflicts with our citizenship? For instance, should the church discipline people for paying taxes that support the military? Or abortion? Or racist policies?

6. Would you submit to the judgment of the church if it sought to discipline you? Why, or why not? Some denominations practiced the ban years ago, putting people out of the church for serious sins. What would Paul say about this practice?.

7. What are some corporate or national sins we participate in? How should the church discipline in these cases?

8. Matthew 18 and 1 Corinthians 6 offer ways of confronting a brother or sister. Talk about your level of ease or unease with this process. Recall not only situations in which someone was confronted, but also think about situations where people suffered because intervention did not happen.

9. Tell stories about discipline you received as a child. Did it serve to bring a "saint" back into the family community, or did it cause further separation?

10. Give each other tips on how to deal with feelings of judgment, revenge, and retribution. Is it ever appropriate to have these feelings? If so, what are we to do with them?

5.
The Freedom to Be Responsible
1 Corinthians 8:1-13

Prepare

1. Read the Bible passage for this session. What are the idols of our day? If they do not really exist, as Paul says, why are they such a threat to the church and to Christians?

2. Notice what Paul is saying about freedom and responsibility. Who are the people in your life who keep you honest? How does your responsibility to the body of Christ compare to your obligations to others, such as family, friends, or coworkers?

3. As you read this session, think about your faith maturity. How mature or immature would you say you are? Why? What would help you mature in your faith?

Share and Pray

1. Tell about the time you were first aware of being responsible for someone besides yourself. Did you resent it or accept it gladly? Did you change your behavior to fulfill your responsibility? If so, how?

2. Paul urges the Corinthians to glorify God in their bodies. In what ways do you celebrate and glorify God in your body? How do you take care of this precious vessel that holds your life and the Holy Spirit? What are some ways you could make changes that would help you to be more healthy in body?

3. Silently reflect on your physical body. Draw an outline of the human body. Put your name in the picture. Using crayons or colored pencils, color the areas to indicate how you feel. For example, you might use red or black to indicate pain in your lower back. Or you might use blue or green to indicate peace and calm in your head and heart area.

4. Give thanks to God for your body and for the ways it serves you. Pray for God's healing in areas of your body that are in pain. If it is appropriate for your group, you might share in prayer by laying on hands and praying for individuals who request it. Pray for the strengthening of individual bodies and the body of Christ, the church.

5. Try memorizing Psalm 100 together if you don't know it by heart already. Creating hand motions or using sign language will help reinforce the words in your mind. To close, recite or read Psalm 100 together.

Christians in Corinth were divided over the issue of sacrificing food to idols. For some it was a matter of freedom—the freedom to do anything they wished, having been freed from Jewish law. Others felt it was a Christian responsibility to stay completely away from infidels.

Today we see the same division over prayer in public schools, conscientious objection, and commitments to marriage. Some people, in order to be free of the confines of a judgmental church, are "privatizing" their faith. They worship alone, they pray alone, they sing alone, they take communion while listening to a televangelist. It is true that Jesus taught us to pray in private. On the other hand his was a public ministry, and he worshiped and prayed in public.

A New Kind of Community

Idol worshipers exist in our day, too. They are the people who feel little obligation to others as long as they obey the laws and mind their own business. Their privacy is a cherished right guaranteed by the Constitution and Bill of Rights. But our society bears the signs of privacy run amuck. People live with a fortress mentality: fearful of others, suspicious of neighbors, cautious about helping people. The role of the church and its members is to be a new kind of community, just as in Paul's time. Its first response to God's grace is to live as the body, tending to the needs of the body and preparing it to be the home for the presence of Christ. God frees us for this liberating work of being a community.

In a society that prizes individualism, as did Corinth, some people think that their actions affect only themselves. They do as they please, even in the church. Paul wrote to remind the church at Corinth that it is the body of Christ, a collection of talents and abilities that make up a whole. To search after their own individual selves would destroy the fabric of the church.

> **The role of the church and its members is to be a new kind of community, just as in Paul's time. Its first response to God's grace is to live as the body, tending to the needs of the body and preparing it to be the home for the presence of Christ.**

I once was fishing with a wise pastor. We were talking about the church and its problems. At a certain point he looked at the net he was using, picked up a knot of the net, and asked me, "What happens when I lift up this knot?" I answered, "The whole net comes up." "Yes, you're right. This is so because knots are connected one with another. The same thing happens in the church; each member is connected to the whole fabric of the church as a knot is connected to the net. When one knot moves right or left, the whole net moves too. We belong one to another."

That pastor was using the net as a metaphor for the body of Jesus Christ. Our "bodies are members of Christ" (1 Cor. 6:15). I am what I am, but I am also what Jesus Christ is. What I do with my body, with my life, I'm doing with Jesus Christ, too (6:12-20). In another letter to the church at Corinth, Paul says we are "always carrying in the body the death of Jesus, so that the life of Jesus may also be made visible in our bodies" (2 Cor. 4:10). In a letter to the Galatian church, he writes, "I carry the marks of Jesus branded on my body" (Gal. 6:17).

Paul is not speaking in a metaphorical way as the pastor did. He is speaking about a visible and concrete presence of Christ in us. For him, the statement that we are identified with the death and resurrection of Jesus Christ is not just a theological affirmation. It is a reality that determines the way we live in the here and now. He is being quite literal when he says, "I have been crucified with Christ; and it is no longer I who live, but it is Christ who lives in me. And the life I now live in the flesh I live by faith in the Son of God" (Gal. 2:19-20).

Mature Faith

We don't belong to ourselves. We are members of the body of Jesus Christ and the Holy Spirit's temple (1 Cor. 6:15-20). And because we are members of the body of Christ, we live sanctified lives dedicated to the Lord (6:12-14). Paul compares our dedication to God to fidelity in marriage (7:1-16). The confines of marriage keep us from sexual immorality. Similarly, faith confines our beliefs to trust in one God who is greater than all gods and all systems of belief. As a member in the body of Christ, we are not lured to other faiths or temptations, just as in a healthy marriage, we are satisfied and fulfilled by one union.

> **A mature person is not the person who holds the truth, but the person who uses the truth with love. There are many people who know a lot about everything, but they know nothing about love. They have good ideas, good insights, good explanations, but without love, they do not know God.**

In chapter 8, Paul notes several ways that faith is mature. First, he notes that faith is not just knowing God in our hearts and minds. It is not enough to hold the truth; it is necessary to use the truth with love. Again we see the difference between human intelligence and God's wisdom: An intelligent person may know a great deal, but a wise person uses intelligence with love to promote life and the neighbor's good. A mature person is not the person who holds the truth, but the person who uses the truth with love. There are many people who know a lot about everything, but they know nothing about love. They have good ideas, good insights, good explanations, but without love, they do not know God.

Secondly, mature faith recognizes that all things belong to God who is the reason for all things (8:4-8). If everything is from God and God is over all, then nothing can be forbidden. Paul illustrates this with food sacrificed to idols, which Jews would have avoided since it was pagan food. But Paul reminds us that food sacrificed to idols is first of all food that is made by God. These verses remind us of Peter's dream in Acts 11 in which Peter has a vision of eating unclean meat at God's command, for nothing that comes from God can be unclean. We cannot control the gods by sacrifices anyway. Our God is sovereign, beyond our control. The New Testament most frequently refers to Christ as Lord, reinforcing the truth that God cannot be plied.

Some Christians not only avoid the practices of other faiths and cultures for fear of being unfaithful to Christ, but will not practice Christian customs from different traditions for the same reason. For instance, many of us grew up believing that we could not go into a Catholic church if we were Protestant or into a Protestant church if we were Catholic, as if all faith did not come from God.

Thirdly, to be mature in faith is to live as an example for others (8:9-13). The sovereignty of God liberates us from competing with rituals and laws for God's attention. However, Paul encourages us to observe the rituals of others with respect, for if they believe we are judging them, they may be forever intimidated from the true knowledge of God. Their confused knowledge of God and the effectiveness of sacrifice already indicate that they are weak and helpless. Only the example, sensitivity, and nurture of the strong can help the weak to have more confidence in God.

> **Paul encourages us to observe the rituals of others with respect, for if they believe we are judging them, they may be forever intimidated from the true knowledge of God.**

Be Careful What You Say or Do

In recent years, Christians have been guilty of condemning people of other faiths instead of strengthening the non-Christian's confidence in God. We perhaps overestimate the power of other religions to influence us and our children. Paul, according to this passage, would encourage more frequent contact, because only in dialogue and friendship can we persuade by example and reason that our God is the only true God.

Of course, it is also easy to be a stumbling block to weak Christians who may follow our example of freedom but not the example of our strong faith. We are like adults who must watch what they say in front of children. A woman told me about the time she said within earshot of a young nephew that she smoked a cigarette with a friend who felt his Christian coworkers were judging him for being a smoker. The woman wanted to show him that smoking or not smoking does not make someone good or bad. The immature, undiscriminating boy learned from his aunt's story that smoking is good. After all, one of his respected elders does it.

The freedom that God bestows on us to talk with others does not give us license to follow our individual whims and desires. In a strange way, the liberty we gain from not having to worry about ritual and law requires greater responsibility on our part for being examples for our brothers and sisters. People who practice a ritual to satisfy the gods have fulfilled all their obligations. It does not matter how they behave once their duty is fulfilled. But the God who assures us that we are loved and releases us from striving for acceptance makes other demands on us, mainly that we are to be the body of Christ in the world and all that that means.

I have a friend who is Quechua (pronounced *Ketch-wa*), an indigenous nation in Ecuador. One day we were talking about their lifestyle, especially their social structure. He explained that they live in communities where decisions, jobs, land ownership, and education are handled by the whole community. I asked him about Quechua attitudes about privacy and personal freedom. At first he didn't understand very well what I was asking. He said: "Privacy for me is to be in my community, with my people. They are me, I am them. We grew up together, we worked together, and we made decisions together. I educated their children and they educated my children. My private space is my community."

"What about personal freedom?" I asked. "Do you feel limited in any aspect?"

"Yes and no. At times I have desired to do this or that, but I thought that it might break up our beautiful community. Then, I decided to give it up out of love for my people."

"And did you feel bad about that?" I asked.

"No! I felt good because I love my people and I wanted to preserve my community as we are: one for all and all for one."

This was his way of saying that he is a member of the body. I am a member of the body, too. What I do has corporate implications. I can promote unity or division with my behavior and actions. As a Christian, I am married to the body of Jesus Christ and, consequently, I am wedded to my brothers and sisters. I am one with them and one with Jesus Christ. My life is connected to others. I can support and be supported, strengthen and be strengthened, love and be loved.

Discuss and Act

1. Read 1 Corinthians 8:1-13 aloud. Poll each other, asking whether each person feels more like an individual in the church or a part of an interdependent group. What responsibilities do you have for each other in the church? To what extent do the people in your congregation carry this out?

2. What examples of unity does Paul use in these passages? What are some others?

3. In 1 Corinthians 10:23, Paul teaches that, while things may indeed be lawful, they may not be beneficial or upbuilding. Name some things in our time that are lawful but not beneficial, nor do they build up the church or individuals.

4. There is a motto that says: "For the glory of God and my neighbor's good." What does this expression mean to you? Are there some things you would do for your neighbor's good that you wouldn't do normally? What does Paul advise in such a case?

5. The author talks about a mature faith. As a group, list criteria for a mature faith. What responsibility do mature Christians have for the nurture of immature Christians? How would you rate your congregation or your covenant group as nurturers?

6. In pairs, talk about which signs of maturity you possess and which you need to work on. Think of a way to gain maturity in one area, and covenant with your partner to work on it.

7. Our pioneer heritage encourages us to be ruggedly individualistic. Paul reminds us, however, that we are called to be aware of ways that our behavior affects others. Where do you see this contradiction in your own life? In what areas of your life do you feel pulled to change your life in order to avoid adversely influencing another?

8. Think of times you have been an insider in a group. Think of times you have been an outsider. Which are you now in your church, where you work, in your community, or in your family? What can your covenant group do to build up the church, making everyone feel like they are part of "the net"?

9. If you know it, sing 'Weave, Weave, Weave Us Together" or "We Are People of God's Peace."

6.
All Things to All People
1 Corinthians 9:1–10:13

Prepare

1. Read 1 Corinthians 9:1–10:13. Think this week about how your freedom is a building block for others, or how it is a stumbling block for them.

2. How many times have you said to yourself, "I can't please everyone. I can't be all things to all people." Yet that is exactly what Paul asks us to do. When have you become like someone in order to help them? What are the dangers of becoming all things to all people?

3. As you read this week, be mindful of the differences between your freedom accorded to you by the government and the freedom you receive as a Christian. Which is more important in your life? Why?

Share and Pray

1. Find a partner and talk about the stumbling blocks in your faith journey at this time. What stands in your way or trips you up as you seek to deepen your faith and commitment? Are you aware of being a stumbling block for others? In what ways? After each of you has shared, pray

silently for each other, asking God for the courage and power to change that which causes others to stumble.

2. Paul says that we will not be tested beyond our strength (1 Cor. 10: 13). Describe a time when you were tested to the limits of your endurance. What got you through? What did you need that you didn't get?

3. You may have seen the bumper sticker that says, "Practice random kindness and senseless acts of beauty." Can you remember a random act of kindness that touched you? At the time, did you know who did it? Were kindness and beauty building blocks for you? If so, how did they increase your faith? Have you committed a random kindness or a senseless act of beauty recently? What could you do this week to commit such acts of kindness and beauty?

4. Offer prayers of thanksgiving for endurance and strength in times of trouble. Recite together or have one person read Romans 5:1-5 as a confession of faith.

A student of mine once said to me: "I am free to smoke, to drink, to dance, to eat all kinds of food. I will never abandon them, even if it scandalizes someone else." I thought for a moment and responded: "If you are free to smoke or drink but can't abstain from them out of love for your brother or sister, you are not free. You are a slave of cigarettes and drink."

North Americans prize their freedom. After all, liberty is one of the basic rights of being human. However, liberty is not absolute. Personal liberty is limited by our neighbor's liberty and rights. And Christian liberty actually makes us slaves of one another through love!

In this letter to the church at Corinth, Paul addresses the theme of personal liberty. He is writing at a time when Corinth was home to many cultures and had little social cohesion. The people felt free to do anything they wished. Christians in Corinth, however, were still deeply tied to Mosaic Law and lived slavishly under religious rules, even though grace and forgiveness were to have replaced the law.

License to Do Whatever?

There is some indication in the letters to Corinth that the church was under the influence of Jewish Christians who were still teaching that the law was necessary to complete the salvation given by Jesus Christ. They taught that faith in Christ plus strict observance of the law produced salvation. The church in Corinth was heavily regulated by laws about the sabbath, dress, meat, drink, the veil, circumcision, and marriage. But Paul says the law does not free us. Jesus Christ frees us from the law to act in love and liberty.

This portion of Paul's letter seems full of mixed messages. We are free. We are slaves. We ought to be all things to all people. What does Paul want us to do? Paul uses examples from his life to demonstrate how he uses his own freedom to restrict his own freedom. He has every right accorded to human beings and every right accorded to him by his salvation in Jesus Christ, but he only exercises those freedoms that will build up others in the faith. He expects the Corinthian church to practice the same kind of self-discipline.

> This portion of Paul's letter seems full of mixed messages. We are free. We are slaves. We ought to be all things to all people. What does Paul want us to do?

For instance, by law a farmer would get a share of the crop he raised, the ox was entitled to some of the grain it threshed, the herder was entitled to a share of the milk the animals produced. In the same way, Paul was entitled to some financial support from the Christians he served. But he chooses not to use this entitlement because it may rankle some Christians and keep them from pursuing the faith.

We do the same thing today, whether we are aware of it or not. While we have freedom of speech for the good of the whole society, the law (also for the good of society) keeps us from saying threatening things or things that would defame someone.

Similarly, freedom of religion allows everyone to believe as they wish, but for the good of everyone, the law prohibits the practice of any religion in places where people cannot dissent, as in a public school. The First Amendment rights of the U.S. Constitution are not a license to do as we wish, if by doing what we wish we infringe upon other people's rights.

How Do You Decide?

What distinguishes the rights of a Christian from the rights of a citizen then, if both are deserving of their freedom? Paul tells us in chapter 9 that freedom for Christians comes from the liberating grace of God. Human rights and civil rights are given by governments and enforced by law. But governments do not liberate us to work at building up the community. Governments compel citizens by enforcing laws and inflicting penalties.

As children of God, on the other hand, we willingly limit our own freedom in order to be building blocks for others. Christians are called to go one better than the fulfillment of the law and operate out of God's grace.

> Governments compel citizens by enforcing laws and inflicting penalties. As children of God, on the other hand, we willingly limit our own freedom in order to be building blocks for others.

What's more, freedoms guaranteed by governments come and go, but God's liberation is available to us all the time. We can be enslaved and know the liberating hand of God. We can be poor and know that God values us and demands much of us. We can live under oppressive regimes and know that the true authority over our lives is a God who liberates.

As if freedom from the law and the rulers of this world is not enough, God frees us from other confinements as well. We are freed from anxiety about the future. With God's assurances, we do not have to worry about our worth. God promises to be present with us, freeing us from fear and self-doubt. And no matter what ridiculous thing we do as "free" people, God will forgive us.

With this sort of confidence, Paul shows how he can enslave himself and still be free. He can assume the slavish life of a servant and still know the freeing gift of God's love. He can apply himself to any work and know that even the least honored work is esteemed by God. He can practice any ritual or law with his friends, knowing that God, who is greater than these, is neither affected nor offended by rituals. He can be silenced and know that God still hears him.

Freed by Grace

Freedom for Paul is not like freedom as the world defines it. Freedom in the world protects us from the control of others and frees us from compulsory service to anyone. The freedom of the gospel, however, does just the opposite. Having been given our freedom by grace, much is demanded of us. Paul feels the responsibility to preach the gospel and win others to it, and to that goal he will enslave himself.

There was a missionary in Africa who had a very Paul-like way of doing his work. He worked in a country that was very poor and made up of many non-Christians. Instead of entering communities with an offer to teach the gospel, this missionary approached local leaders with an offer to provide a service they needed. If they needed clean water, he dug a well. If their herds were weak, he gave them vaccines. If they needed farming equipment, he got it for them. And if the people were hungry, be helped them get food. The missionary lived among the people, taking part in their life and doing his work without saying a word about the gospel of Jesus Christ.

After months of working together, the people asked him, "Why did you come here to work with us? Why did you make such a personal sacrifice to come to this miserable place?" This was their first invitation to talk about his faith, but he said only a little. He told them that he knew they needed water and that his God sent him. Sometime later, the people made another invitation. They asked, "Tell us about the God who would send someone to help us." And he told them a little more.

Never compelled by threats of eternal punishment or even the loss of water if they did not convert, the people became very curious about the missionary's gracious God. Over the course of several years, the missionary told them about Jesus and the steadfast love of God. And over years, their faith was built up until they believed.

Some Christians would be dubious of a missionary who seemed to lack enthusiasm for his convictions. He ate, worked, and worshiped with them, almost as if he accepted their beliefs and practice. How could he win converts if he was simply all things to all people? To the people at home, it appeared that he had been missionized by the people to whom he ministered.

All for the Sake of the Gospel

Each disciple of the gospel is compelled or required to do something for God: become weak to win the weak, be like the unfaithful in order to persuade them. For the sake of the gospel, we must become all things to all people.

The student who was enslaved to cigarettes and alcohol in the beginning of this chapter is like the Christian who wraps himself in the Bible and boasts about his superior faith as though he alone knows the freedom of the gospel. True freedom is the knowledge of forgiveness—Paul must have been forgiven for persecuting Jews—and the desire to serve God. Can people be truly free if they follow the law conscientiously but feel guilty because they are not perfect?

> **As Christians we are free to love, to promote life and justice and peace. As Christians we have a commitment to love ourselves as well as our neighbors. This is the parameter for our liberty.**

As Christians we are free to love, to promote life and justice and peace. As Christians we have a commitment to love ourselves as well as our neighbors. This is the parameter for our liberty. The body of Christ is composed of free members, enslaved to one another through love of Jesus Christ. Only when there is liberty among members is there maturity, spiritual growth, and edification.

Discuss and Act

1. Read 1 Corinthians 9. What would it mean to actually apply the principles in 9:19-23? Tell about a time you tried to be all things to all people.

2. Talk about your freedoms as a citizen of a country and your freedoms as members of the body of Christ. Where do they conflict? What do you do when they clash? Which kind of freedom is more important to you?

3. In groups of two or three, or as a large group, tell about ways that you have been a building block. Then tell how you have been a stumbling block to would-be Christians.

4. How is your congregation or covenant group involved in building up the church and being all things to all people? What should it be doing that it is not? Make a list of ideas for building up the church. Choose your top three or four and share them with the pastor.

5. What are the dangers of being all things to all people? How can we avoid these dangers?

6. How would you convince someone that Paul makes sense when he says freedom is slavery and slavery is freedom? Divide into two groups; one is to be convinced and the other is to do the convincing. Work separately to come up with arguments. Then come together to present your cases.

7. Invite a progress report about the project proposed in sessions 1 and 2. Work further on details to carry out the project.

7. Sharing Our Lives
1 Corinthians 11:17-34

Prepare

1. Read 1 Corinthians 11:17-34. As you read, think about how you partake of communion. What does it mean for you? Why do you do it?
2. Prepare something to share at a communion service with your covenant group. Consider writing a short prayer, singing a hymn, sharing a short reading, offering a kindness to someone in the group, or presenting one of your gifts for the benefit of others.
3. How do you prepare daily in order to be ready to go to the Lord's Supper?

Share and Pray

1. Share the story of a special communion service you participated in. Tell your group where you were, what the circumstances were, why it was special, and what impact it had on your life.
2. Bring hymnals to your group meeting and share your favorite communion hymns. Sing them or read particular verses and tell why they are special. As a group, select one hymn to prepare for sharing communion as a closing.

3. What do these words mean to you: "This is my body that is broken for you. Do this in remembrance of me" and "This is the new covenant in my blood. Do this, as often as you drink it, in remembrance of me"?
4. What idols tempt us today as a society? What idols tempt you?
5. As an act of "communion" with one another, go around the circle and invite each person to share a word of new life and affirmation with the person next to them. Then share a simple meal of bread and juice with one another. Use the communion resources found in the Resource Pages or in your hymnal or worship book as a guide, along with 1 Corinthians 11:23-26.

The Rarámuri is an indigenous nation in Mexico. They have a special way of understanding life together. They say the Rarámuri didn't create all things. God did it for them to give them food and a way to share with needy people. If they hoard food, neglecting to help the poor, they are ungrateful to God because the way to give thanks is to share (Ricardo Robles, *Rostros Indios de Dios* 33-37).

Paul thinks of communion and worship in the same way. Communion is the willingness to share gifts, goods, and life. For him, communion is neither an ordinary meal nor simply a spiritual feeling. It is an action, a willingness to come together to share common goods, blessings, joys, and concerns. Communion is not a Sunday morning issue, but a lifestyle for the whole week.

> **Communion is neither an ordinary meal nor simply a spiritual feeling. It is an action, a willingness to come together to share common goods, blessings, joys, and concerns. Communion is not a Sunday morning issue, but a lifestyle for the whole week.**

By the time Paul wrote to the Corinthians, worship and communion were no longer used to bring the church together. Paul said, "When you come together as a church, I hear that there are divisions among you" (11:18). Instead of coming to commune, putting differences aside, people were coming to be with this or that faction.

The church had become a collection of cliques that would not communicate or share the life of the church with each other.

The Whole Body of Christ

For Paul, Christians must be in communion, because only when they work together do they become the whole body of Christ, which they commemorate each time they share the cup (10:16), the bread (v. 16), and worship (v. 20). When people share feelings and actions and gifts in something together, they are in communion. Christians share the fact that they are saved through the same cross, death, and resurrection of Jesus. Furthermore, all Christians share the honor of representing Christ in the world. To be sure, we are all different; we are his body, hands, and feet that remain in this world. We are inseparably linked together as one. We are in communion.

In 1 Corinthians, Paul tells us how people in communion act, or don't act. We respect those in the body of Christ who are different (11:17-18), avoiding the temptation to share only with those who are the same as we are. We look out for the needs of others (vv. 21-22), not just our own needs. We examine our own failings before we judge others (v. 28). And we worship together, aware that we must wait on others so that together we make a whole. Real communion is established when we willingly share our whole lives, including belongings, abilities, skills, gifts, and time. Only when we have this attitude can we participate properly in breaking bread (vv. 23-24). Paul says that those who "eat and drink without discerning the body, eat and drink judgment against themselves" (v. 29).

> By breaking bread and drinking the cup, we participate in the sacrifice, we remember Christ, and we proclaim the saving blood of Jesus for all. Every act of communion, every sacrifice, every gesture of care toward brothers and sisters proclaims the power of Christ.

We often interpret "discerning the body" to mean we must understand that the broken bread is the body of Christ broken for our redemption. But what Paul really wants us to understand is that each time we partake in the breaking of bread, we experience anew the reconciliation accomplished by Christ's death and resurrection. If the people have not discerned that the church as the body of Christ needs reconciliation, and if alienation remains as it seems to have in the Corinthian church, then the people have made a mockery of Christ's sacrifice.

In this case, Corinthian Christians were experiencing deep alienation. They were divided and unwilling to share even the most basic act of eating together: "When the time comes to eat, each of you goes ahead with your own supper, and one goes hungry and another becomes drunk" (v. 21). Not only did they fail to take the commemoration of Jesus' sacrifice seriously, they failed to care for brothers and sisters, the very mission Jesus left for us. Paul actually attributes weakness, illness, and death to the fact that people were participating in the Lord's Supper without the willingness to share what they had. Many of them were already weak and ill, and some had died (vv. 29-30).

Reconciled to One Another

Before the reenactment of the Lord's Supper in the Church of the Brethren, deacons used to prepare members by visiting each one to ask if he or she was reconciled with everyone in the church. Members were given a chance to renew their baptismal vows and make amends for anything that alienated them from the body of Christ. If reconciliation could not be achieved, churches were known to have postponed the love feast. In one congregation a woman wore a hat, which was an offense to the people who took seriously the guidance of the church to live and dress plainly. In the deacon visit, the deacons asked her not to wear the hat anymore and be reconciled to the congregation or to remove herself from the fellowship. She chose to remove herself. If she had chosen to stay and to keep the hat, the rift would have delayed the love feast. The church has long since ended this style of harsh discipline, but not without consequence. We, like the Corinthians, have forgotten the centrality of reconciliation in communion.

Jesus' sacrifice for our sakes, which we celebrate in communion, is the model for the sacrifices we make for each other. By breaking bread and drinking the cup, we participate in the sacrifice (10:16), we remember Christ (11:24-25), and we proclaim the saving blood of Jesus for all (11:26). Every act of communion, every sacrifice, every gesture of care toward brothers and sisters proclaims the power of Christ.

As long as the Corinthian church was divided and careless, they were unable to proclaim Christ. From Paul's description, the Corinthians seemed oblivious to the erosion in the community. Perhaps they were accustomed to a variety of cultural expressions of praise and let everyone do their own thing. Perhaps they had grown tolerant of the diversity and paid no attention to what others were doing. Are we as nonchalant about our devotion? Do we prepare ourselves for worship and sacrifice, or have we become like the Corinthians? Do we pay attention to the way the church works together, or do we merely come to communion to get out of it what we need personally?

The northeast part of Brazil is a dry region. Bit by bit, it got worse. For more than a year they had no rain. Water and food were scarce and expensive. People who live in that region are the poorest people in Brazil. In order to find better places to work and earn money to survive, many men left the region and their families, going south. The women they left behind were called "dry widows" (abandoned because of the drought).

During that long dry season, a television reporter interviewed one of the "widows" who had three boys. He was very impressed by the poverty in her house. For more than a week they had nothing to eat. He went to the store, bought some food, and returned to the house. The reporter gave the food to the mother. She looked at the food, smiled, thanked him, took half of the food, and went out. In a few minutes she returned smiling. The reporter asked: "What did you do with the food?" "I shared it with my neighbor," she said. "She is a dry widow like me. She is in the same situation. How could I eat this food knowing that she had nothing to eat?"

Sharing Goods, Gifts, and Life

Communion is not communion without sharing. Christians have to share goods, gifts, and life. Corinth's church had a problem in this area. They celebrated the agape meal (love feast) but did not have the interest in waiting to share with those who were hungry (11:33-34). Their own appetites were symbolic of self-centeredness and division in the body. When they met to share the Lord's Supper, some people took more food than they needed, and some had no food to eat at all. The congregation was denying the real meaning of the meal, which is to come together.

The Lord's Supper is more than a symbol. It is a concrete way to say that we are willing to share our lives with others just as Jesus Christ did. To share life is to share our blood, sweat, and tears, our food, and our gifts. When I share my goods, my money, my gifts, I am sharing my very life. I'm sharing what I have produced by my own labor. To give is not just a commercial transaction. When I share what I have, I'm sharing my life and I'm able to say like Jesus: "This is my body which is given for you." This is a real and practical way to experience the reality of the Lord's Supper.

When we don't share what we have, what we are, what we suffer or enjoy, there is no communion. Jesus Christ shared his whole life and body. Likewise, it is impossible to be a Christian person alone, without communion with others, without sharing needs, joys, and concerns. Our communion with God is expressed in our communion with others. No one has true communion with God if there is no true communion with brothers and sisters.

> **Our communion with God is expressed in our communion with others. No one has true communion with God if there is no true communion with brothers and sisters.**

Discuss and Act

1. Read 1 Corinthians 11:17-34. Share some of your personal reflections about the way you partake in communion. What does it mean? Why do you do it?

2. How does your church life resemble communion every day? How do you share your talents and resources between one communion and the next? Look at your congregational budget. Where do the resources go? Do they support the upbuilding of the community? Do they represent a shared life in the church?

3. Is communion in your church mainly for individuals or for the congregation? Do you genuinely enjoy being together? Does communion seem like an obligation? Why? If the practice of sharing is not part of your communion, suggest ways that people could share as part of the commemoration.

4. Do you see "illness" in churches that do not have a healthy communion? What kinds of "illnesses" are the result of insincere communion? Which of these have you experienced? What can be done to remedy the disease?

5. Usually the bread and the cup remind us of Jesus' great sacrifice on our behalf. After reading this chapter, will the bread and cup remind you of our need for reconciliation? How has your view of communion changed?

6. In the past, deacons visited each member of the congregation to reconcile any differences between members before everyone gathered for communion. Should we do something like this today? How would it benefit us? Why do you suppose they stopped doing it?

8. Many Gifts, One Spirit

1 Corinthians 12:1-31; 14:1-40

Prepare

1. Read 1 Corinthians 12 and 14. Use the method described in the session to discern your own gifts. Think of the things you have done for others. Narrow the list to the things that made you feel good. Narrow it again to the things that made others feel good. These are your gifts.

2. Practice calling out the gifts in others. Think about the talents of the people in your covenant group. Make a point to encourage people in their gifts during the remaining weeks of this study and after.

3. Think about the difference between unity and uniformity. In what ways do you try to conform to what others are thinking and doing? In what ways do you develop your own gifts to complement the gifts of others?

Share and Pray

1. When you were young, what did you want to be when you grew up?

2. What one talent or gift would you like to have that you don't have at this time?

3. Paul affirms that in this community of faith, the Corinthians "are not lacking in any spiritual gift" (1 Cor. 1:7). Together, make a list of the many gifts found in individuals in your covenant group and in your congregation. Use your gifts list as a prayer resource for thanksgiving.

4. Think carefully about your God-given gifts. What gifts do you bring to your covenant group? Name one or two special gifts that each member brings to your group. When do your gifts make you a leader in your group? When you are discussing? Singing? Worshiping? Taking action? What gifts do you bring to your church and to the community?

5. Offer prayers for each other, and for God to nurture and call forth the gifts of individuals in the group and others in the church community.

6. As a closing prayer of commitment, sing the hymn, "Take My Life, and Let It Be" or "Have Thine Own Way, Lord," which can be found online or in many hymnals.

7. Close with the prayer "Our Gifts Are Gifts of Hope," found in the Resource Pages.

Sebastiana was an old woman with a dangerous health problem that was getting worse. One day the doctor said, "Sebastiana, you have to stay in bed day and night. The only walking you can do is from your bed to your bathroom and back." She called me crying and depressed. She said to me, "I'm not able to go to church anymore! I have to stay at home, doing nothing. The doctors have declared me useless."

Our church prayed for her and with her, but her feelings of uselessness remained. Several times I visited her, and little by little I discovered that she was not useless. She had the strong gift of compassion, one of the gifts Paul mentions in Romans 12, the parallel passage to 1 Corinthian 12. She had a spiritual ability to suffer with others, to weep with those who weep (Rom. 12:15), to give consolation. I began to ask God for a way Sebastiana could continue to use this gift. One night when I couldn't sleep, God gave me the answer: Put a phone beside her bed and share her number with others so that she can pray with those who are in trouble.

When I proposed it to her, she rejoiced but was scared. She was thrilled at the opportunity to do something to help others, but she was doubtful about her ability to do it. I taught her what the Bible says about spiritual gifts, and at last she accepted the challenge. We put a voice message on her phone that asked callers to leave their numbers if they wanted Sebastiana to pray with them. The church printed flyers announcing this service, and daily the number of calls increased. One day, the phone company called us to find out why the telephones were so busy. In the space of two years, the church became known as Sebastiana's church. The whole city knew and used Sebastiana's gift.

All Receive Spiritual Gifts

Sebastiana illustrates that God gives everyone abilities to serve others even when we think we are useless. Our talents are not merely our gift to God. God is the source of our gifts. By attributing all gifts to the three parts of the Trinity, Paul emphasizes that our gifts come from God: "Now there are varieties of gifts, but the same Spirit; and there are varieties of services, but the same Lord; and there are varieties of activities, but it is the same God who activates all of them in everyone" (1 Cor. 12:4-6). In three ways Paul says that there is a unique source for gifts, services, and activities.

The gifts that God gives—discernment, tongues, interpretation, healing, miracles, prophecy, wisdom, knowledge, and faith—do not all go to the same person. There are no super-Christians who can do it all. God spreads the gifts around so that each person has a talent to contribute and each person's talent is different from the next person's.

All Christians have spiritual gifts. God gives to each of us a special ability to do something in the body of Christ, the church. But one of the great problems that modern Christians have is identifying what gift they have. If you are one who wonders what gift you have for the church, try looking back and examining all the things that you have done to serve others. Next, identify which activities made you feel good when you did them. Then identify the kinds of activities people appreciated when you did them. Find out what you do that makes you and others feel good—that is your spiritual gift. Exercise it!

> **All Christians have spiritual gifts. God gives to each of us a special ability to do something in the body of Christ, the church. But one of the great problems that modern Christians have is identifying what gift they have.**

God gives a variety of gifts to the members of the body of Jesus Christ in order to produce unity, not uniformity. "To each is given the manifestation of the Spirit for the common good" (v. 7). The sum of our diversity equals the whole body of Jesus Christ. We spend most of our lives conforming to laws, styles, trends, and attitudes. But the church needs our uniqueness, not our conformity. While differences can divide, they can also be used for mutual benefit. We are like the ingredients in a loaf of bread, the players on a team, or the parts of a machine.

Spiritual Gifts Bring Unity to the Church

No one can say that because they are different they don't belong to the body. Every Christian belongs to the body of Jesus Christ and has a gift to promote the unity. Alone our gifts mean very little, but united with the gifts of others, they are very powerful. Each spiritual gift has to work in conjunction and coordination with other gifts, because each one depends on the other. The evangelist needs the pastor, the pastor needs the comforter, the comforter needs the exhorter, and so on. Paul writes to the church in Ephesus, saying "the whole body, joined and knit together by every ligament with which it is equipped, as each part is working properly, promotes the body's growth" (Eph. 4:16). When we avoid working together, we weaken the whole body.

Try to imagine a pastor who embodies all the gifts Paul lists and a congregation that practices none of them. We often expect pastors to be all things. If there are such pastors, they are used up and burned out in no time. And the congregations that leave all talents to the pastor are dull and unimaginative. In Paul's analogy of the body, the church with the super-pastor and the inactive congregation is like the diseased body whose organs are failing but whose heart is still strong. A body can last that way a while, but the heart cannot work alone forever.

And even the active congregation with many gifts may misuse them. The purpose of gifts is to edify the body, to build it up. Prophecy, tongues, wisdom, healing, knowledge, and interpretation are all gifts equal in worth. But sometimes we value one more than another. Paul points out in chapter 14 that speaking in tongues, because it seems miraculous, is valued more than plain prophecy or preaching. We easily fall into the trap of competing and judging in the church until the gifts that should bind us together are tearing us apart. Paul reminds us that all gifts are valuable in different ways. The gift of tongues is a valuable way to reach unbelievers, but it is less effective in reaching the already committed. Here preaching is much more powerful.

In our time we may find special ministries to young people, deaf ministries, programs for singles, or service to the needy more glamorous than the typical weekly congregational ministry. But none of us would go a week without regular worship services. It is a misuse of our talents to neglect the ordinary for something more spectacular.

Variety in religious life is evident everywhere. Not only do we serve God and others with varied talents, we express ourselves in worship in a variety of ways. The same Spirit promotes different ways of worshiping God. Variety in worship is also a sign of a healthy body, a unified but not uniform church. Different styles in liturgy are expressions of God's power and creativity. When the Holy Spirit leads, no one can predict what will happen, because the Spirit is like a wind, and "the wind blows where it chooses, and you hear the sound of it, but you do not know where it comes from or where it goes" (John 3:8).

In Corinth's church there was no order of worship as we have today. In Corinth people began to come to worship to show off their gifts, trying to convince others that they were more spiritual because they had the best gift. It created "spiritual competition" and disorder in the church. They were speaking all at the same time, and they were arguing that they were led by the Spirit to do so (14:27, 30-31). But Paul says that God wants order and not confusion (v. 33).

> **Variety in worship is a sign of a healthy body, a unified but not uniform church. Different styles in liturgy are expressions of God's power and creativity. When the Holy Spirit leads, no one can predict what will happen.**

Variety Is Good

Theologian and church historian Dale Brown notes in his book *Flamed by the Spirit* that "whenever any fundamental doctrine of the faith is neglected, a movement will usually emerge to help revive that particular emphasis for the entire church." When we neglect strong preaching as the Corinthian church did, someone like Paul comes along to remedy the imbalance. And in our generation, when we have neglected the spiritual life, charismatic and Spirit-filled movements have come along to fix our lopsided, staid worship.

Brown remembers, even as a child, needing a balance between charisma and disciplined worship. His family crossed town each Sunday to go to their unassuming, quietistic church. As they made their way back home, his father would stop the car in front of a Pentecostal church, whose service lasted long after other churches adjourned. The family remained in the car with the windows down to drink in the deeply spiritual music and preaching, so unlike their own church. Slightly skeptical of the emotionalism of the Pentecostal tradition, they nonetheless needed the depth of experience it offered to complement the practices of their own tradition.

The ideal, however, is for each congregation to embody a variety of gifts. And one of the gifts in the church is the practice of identifying gifts in others and calling them out. There is a great deal of risk in offering our talents, even if we know they come from God. We fear the criticism of others or suffer from very low self-esteem. But when others encourage us in a spirit of love without judging, we can share more freely. We need to examine our churches to see whether they are places where God can be praised by the talents of all, or whether there is only room for professionals, prodigies, geniuses, and the wealthy.

Our culture is not so unlike Corinthian culture of the first century. Social cohesion is eroding, ethnic groups live under great tension, and leadership is lacking. A competitive spirit causes people to be concerned only for themselves. We are suspicious of each other and live fearfully behind fences, locks, and alarm systems. Now, as much as at any other time, we need the gifts and talents of everyone to build up the body. Now is the time to call out the diverse gifts of our Sebastianas and become the whole body of Christ.

Discuss and Act

1. Look over the scripture together. For fun, pass out scratch paper and ask each person to draw a body made up entirely of ears, or a body of arms, or another body part mentioned in 1 Corinthians 12. Share your drawings.

2. What gifts are lacking in your congregation? What would make your worship or your life together more balanced?

3. We often dislike other church traditions. If we are charismatic, we dislike standard preaching and teaching. If we come from a tradition that uses preaching and teaching, we are skeptical about charismatic churches. Compare your church to another type of group, such as employees in a store, workers in a manufacturing plant, or farm workers. How are they alike? How are they different? How important is balance and variety in each?

4. The author talks about the way we treat pastors, often requiring that they perform all aspects of ministry for a congregation. What do you expect from a minister? What ministry do you expect from church members? What is your pastor's strongest gift? Who in the congregation can provide ministries that complement the pastor's?

5. How do we get unity in the church when everyone is developing his or her own gift? Talk about times when your church has had many gifted people but very little cohesion. How can we create unity from our many talents and capabilities? Which is harder in your estimation—unity or conformity? Why?

6. How does your congregation recognize the ordinary but important gifts of its members? Have you ever felt as though your gift was not as important as someone else's? Make a list of gifts. Which ones are necessary to the life of the church? Which ones are enriching but not truly necessary? Which list is made up of ordinary gifts? What does this exercise tell you about the way we value gifts in our churches?

7. Offer prayers for each other that God will nurture and call forth the gifts of individuals in the group and others in the church community. Close by singing "Many Gifts, One Spirit," found online and in many hymnals.

9. The Greatest of These Is Love

1 Corinthians 13:1-13

Prepare

1. Read 1 Corinthians 13:1-13. This passage is often used in wedding services. Read it every day this week (maybe even memorize it!), thinking about what it means for your congregation, your family, and your work place.

2. If love is an action, not just a feeling, make a list of things you are doing to love others. What are you doing especially for your "enemies" or people you dislike?

3. Love is God's gift for us to do. Think of a time that you knew the love you gave had to come from somewhere other than yourself.

Share and Pray

1. What is your definition of love at this time in your life? Describe a recent experience when you felt truly loved. How has your concept of love changed over time?

2. When you were a child, who loved you? How did those who loved you express this love? How did it affect you?

3. Share your favorite scripture passages mentioning or describing some aspect of love. Read some or all of them aloud to one another.

4. What are your favorite love songs? What are your favorite hymns about love? What are your favorite poems about love? What is your favorite love story, book, or movie?

5. In this great chapter on love, Paul tells us what love is and what love is not. In groups of two or three, rewrite this passage using new understandings and definitions. Read your group's work to the whole group.

6. Offer prayers of celebration to God for ways you have been loved and ways God has called you to love others. Seek God's guidance in discovering ways to love those who are hard to love.

7. Sing "Love Divine, All Loves Excelling" (found online and in most hymnals), along with other favorite songs about God's love. If you prefer, invite someone to read the lyrics aloud as the group sits silently, prayerfully, with eyes closed.

Roberto was the pastor of a small church and a seminary teacher. One day he discovered that the former pastor, Carlos, who still attended that congregation, had made some disparaging comments about him to the seminary president.

When Roberto heard the charges, he immediately became very anxious about his family, his finances, his profession, and his friendships. His first reaction was to take his wife with him to Carlos' house and ask if he had truly said these things. When Carlos answered in an evasive way, Roberto began to angrily accuse him of being disloyal, cynical, a wolf masquerading as a lamb, and a Judas.

When he finished he said good-bye and left, giving Carlos no chance to say anything. After that, Roberto came to my house and told me what he had done. I listened carefully and then told him that he had to return to Carlos to give him a chance to tell why he did what he did. But Roberto said he would never do that.

When Roberto returned to his house, there were flowers on the table with a brief message: "I love you, my pastor. I apologize for what happened. Can you forgive me? I invite you and your wife to come to my house for dinner with us today." And it was signed by Carlos. In the end, Roberto went to Carlos' house and their strong friendship was repaired.

Love Is an Action

This is an example of loving one's neighbor when love is not so easy. It shows that love is not just a feeling that can be conjured up or forced. It is an action. We love not only when we feel good about someone, but when we don't feel love for them; yet we know we must act lovingly.

The act of loving works even when we are dealing with true enemies, not just neighbors. Gandhi based the whole movement for India's liberation from the British on the belief that love could be used to overcome evil. He called it *truth force* or *love force*, and held up Jesus as a model for acting lovingly toward enemies.

We don't have to do grand things to love a neighbor. Small gestures that meet everyday needs are actions of love. And we can always find small things to do for others, even if it is as simple as carrying something for someone, helping neighbors move, fixing an appliance, exchanging recipes, cleaning for someone who is sick or disabled, caring for a friend's children from time to time, remembering a birthday, or saying "I appreciate what you did."

> **We don't have to do grand things to love a neighbor. Small gestures that meet everyday needs are actions of love.**

In his letter to Corinth, Paul deals with conflicts that were tearing the church apart. Christians were competing among themselves to show who had the greatest spiritual gifts. Some claimed that prophecy was best, others believed God favored Christians who had the gift of tongues. Still others thought that faith and compassion were the best gifts. Paul dampens all of their illusions, saying none of these are as important as the gift of love. Unless gifts are motivated out of love, they are worthless.

Recall our study of divine wisdom and human wisdom. Human wisdom is what we can know in the natural world. But divine wisdom is knowledge that God gives. God's logic is what makes divine wisdom different from human wisdom. And love is what makes divine action different from human action. Without love our actions have no meaning. In Paul's description of what love is, he never refers to love as a frame of mind or a feeling. It is an action—kindness, patience, endurance, and modesty.

Love Defined

Beginning in verse 4, Paul defines love. He says that love is patient, kind, and never-ending. Love is not envious, boastful, arrogant, rude, irritable, or resentful. Try applying these descriptions to Corinthian Christians! There was no patience, people were rude, envious, arrogant, and irritable. All of this was happening in the name of spirituality, spiritual gifts, and divine wisdom.

Corinth's Christians were divided into groups, accusing one another, unwilling to understand one another, and unwilling to forgive. Love forgives (v. 6), love bears all things, love believes all things, love hopes all things, and love endures all things (v. 7). As a divine act, love is given by God for us to do. But the Corinthians arrogantly took credit for their spiritual prowess and mistook their own meager deeds for divine ones. They did not understand that for actions to be divinely inspired, they had to be founded in love.

> **The world tells us that love is something we deserve, and something we feel for people who are like us and attracted to us. But just as Paul turned wisdom upside down, he turns love upside down. It is not something we deserve, but something we need.**

The idea of doing everything out of love feels awkward to us. The logic of the world tells us that love is something we deserve, and something we feel for people who are like us and attracted to us. But just as Paul turned wisdom upside down, he turns love upside down. It is not something we deserve, but something we need. God gives love freely even when we don't deserve it. All that God does is based on love for us. We ought also to let love be the reason for everything that we do.

Acts of love are acts in favor of my neighbor that promote life. Jesus Christ loved us. He came (action), lived with us (action), suffered as we suffer (action), died (action), and was resurrected (action). The Bible says that God so loved the world that God gave a Son (action). In his first letter, John says: "How does God's love abide in anyone who has the world's goods and sees a brother or sister in need and yet refuses help? . . . Let us love, not in word or speech, but in truth and action" (1 John 3:17-18).

The way to love others, especially enemies, is to do something for them, even when we don't feel love. This is the reason the psalmist asks God to "prepare a table before me in the presence of my enemies" (Psalm 23:5). The way to take down the barriers that obstruct communion is to search out our enemies and do something for them. Jesus taught in Matthew 18 that we must go to the one who offends us to talk with them, to reconcile with them.

Self-examination

We cannot point our fingers at the failings of the Corinthians without examining ourselves for the same weaknesses. We also fall into judging the strength and authenticity of the faith of others instead of acting in love. As congregations we argue over the pastor's sermons, the organist's performance, and the views of the Sunday school teacher. We identify our church as evangelical, progressive, conservative, traditional, or apostolic, as though our church was doing things the right way and all others were misguided.

Moreover, we are guilty of arrogance in our actions. Rather than acting out of the gift of God's love that makes us want to do the good and loving thing, we too often try to offer our good deeds in exchange for God's love. In our striving to find favor, we compete with others and climb over them to get to the top. We try to be present wherever there is need in order to earn justification. We strive to do the impossible: Work out our salvation.

We are as misguided as the Corinthians, but we are also as gifted as they were and very capable of acting out of love. We must examine our motives and call ourselves back to divine wisdom and divine action. We do not have to act merely out of guilt or ambition to be saved. We can rejoice in the truth that God loves us and frees us to give the gift of love to others.

Love Is a Leveler

Fraught with civil and religious unrest in their country, Nigerian Christians know the meaning of the God-given freedom to love. For years, hatred has grown between Christians and Muslims in Nigeria. At the height of tensions, rioting erupted and radical Muslims burned down more than one hundred churches. Then in retaliation, a group of Christians destroyed three mosques. With scores of churches in smoldering ruin, Christians called a meeting of their leaders to decide whether to rebuild or whether to move out of the danger zone.

Love is a leveler. It erases the distinctions between us and assumes that everyone, no matter who he or she is, is worthy of love.

The young people of the region heard of the meeting and feared that the churches would retreat, avoiding any further conflict. So they went to the leaders in advance of the meeting and asked permission to organize prayer and fasting in the region, hoping to impart courage to the leaders in their decision making. The leaders granted permission and for two weeks the people prayed and fasted.

At the end of the leaders' meeting, a spokesperson emerged with the news. Two things had been decided. First, congregations would begin immediately to gather funds to build new churches where the old ones had stood. Second, the first money raised would be used to replace the mosques that Christians had destroyed.

Loving action not only restored the churches, it opened up communications between Christians and Muslims, prompted conversions, and eased the tensions that were destroying the society. One Muslim was so overcome by the power of his enemies' action that he wanted to know more about the God who could inspire such love.

Paul's beautiful lesson on love is not just poetic; it is crucial to his teaching on unity. Competition and individualism, like Paul saw in Corinth and like we see in our churches, emphasize the differences between people. Some people in the church at Corinth thought they were better than others, refusing to associate with them at meals and worship. Today, we have the same division in churches.

But love is a leveler. It erases the distinctions between us and assumes that everyone, no matter who he or she is, is worthy of love. After all, the unity of the body of Christ is founded on God's most profound act of love: sending Jesus Christ, a poor carpenter and minister, who gave his own life for us even when we didn't deserve it. We also ought to act in love toward one another.

Discuss and Act

1. Read 1 Corinthians 13 aloud. Notice the gifts Paul mentions in the first paragraph: tongues, joyful noise, prophecy, and strong faith. These are the gifts he mentions in chapter 12 that are highly valued, but worthless without love. God gives each of us gifts—extraordinary ones and ordinary ones—but God gives everyone the gift of love, the greatest gift of all. How do you use your gift of love? How will love enhance your individual gifts?

2. Paul describes love as an action rather than a feeling. In fact, love almost sounds like a person in verses 4-7. Read these verses, substituting your own name in the place of "it." Then in groups of two or three, discuss what you are doing to love others or what, perhaps, you need to do.

3. Love is sometimes difficult, especially when it comes to loving people we don't like. Talk about a time when a loving action helped you overcome your dislike or hatred for another person. How did love change the way you felt about the person? Are you able to give love to someone and at the same time express your anger? How so?

4. Why do you think Paul believes love is greater than faith and hope?

5. What does it mean to see in a mirror dimly? What mystifying questions of faith would you like to see resolved? What keeps you going even though the answers are unattainable? How does love help you endure?

6. Paul writes this chapter of Corinthians presumably because the church there was quarreling and competing. How does your congregation compare to the Corinthian church? Is it unified and loving or divided and quarrelsome? How can God's gift of love help us overcome even the most controversial divisions? Is there a limit to the love you are able to give? Why?

7. Turn to "Faith, Hope, and Love" in the Resource Pages and read this together as your closing prayer.

10.
Follow the Dream
1 Corinthians 15:1-58

Prepare

1. Read 1 Corinthians 15. What was your earliest understanding of life after death? What do you believe now about eternal life? What difference does it make to you that Jesus died and was resurrected? What do you find most comforting about verses 50-58?

2. As you read this session, think about how you are a part of Jesus' resurrection. How have you helped carry on Jesus' mission of reconciliation?

3. Review this ten-session study of Christian unity in your mind this week. What have you learned about your group or congregation? What have you learned about yourself? What hopes has this study inspired in you? What questions remain unanswered?

Share and Pray

1. What stands out to you as a symbol or sign of new life?

2. Share a meaningful Easter memory. What are your family Easter traditions? How about your church's traditions? What do you remember about Easter when you were growing up?

3. What is your favorite Easter hymn? If your group sings, sing several of the hymns as people share about them.

4. What was your earliest understanding of life after death? What do you believe now about eternal life? If your understandings have changed, what accounts for that change?

5. What do you find most comforting about 1 Corinthians 15:50-58?

6. Sing or read Natalie Sleeth's "In the Bulb There Is a Flower," which is a hymn of joy and resurrection. You can find it online or in many hymnals.

7. As you prepare to conclude this study, reflect on your experience. What has been especially meaningful for you in this time? What questions remain? What do you want to say to your brothers and sisters about your time together?

8. Give thanks to God: for each other, for gifts and talents to serve others, for a community that honors the uniqueness of each person, for a community that cares enough to challenge you when you stray into harmful areas, for reconciliation to heal brokenness.

9. For closing, stand in a circle and pray together "New Shoots," found in the Resource Pages. Covenant to continue praying for each other and checking in with one another during the coming weeks.

Oscar Romero was the Archbishop of San Salvador, El Salvador, in the 1970s. A Christian committed to his neighbors in their need and in their struggle for justice and peace, he showed love for his people in many concrete actions. Living in the midst of a society marked by violence and death, his religious beliefs gave him hope. His conviction about the truth of the resurrection was a consolation for him and for his people.

But he faced enormous problems. Some people in power didn't like what he was saying and doing. They didn't like his ministry to the poor and his criticisms of the government. They threatened him with death, but even that didn't faze him. All the while, Romero became more and more involved in the struggle for justice and peace. As the tension mounted, he said, "If they kill me, I will be resurrected in the Salvadoran people."

They did kill him as he raised the cup in mass. And he was resurrected in his people who worked all the harder for justice. As a living man, Romero was one voice speaking and two hands doing. But the resurrected Romero became a multitude of voices and hands. Believing that people would carry on the struggle after his death gave him the power and courage to give his own life for his people.

What Is Resurrection?

Paul wrote to the Corinthian church about resurrection. Apparently there was some confusion among Corinthian Christians about different doctrines of resurrection. Some preachers were teaching that there would be no future resurrection of the dead (vv. 12-14). Resurrection for them seemed far out, quite impossible. Others were saying that resurrection is not bodily. They believed in the immortality of the soul, but could not imagine the body rising. To them resurrection was a metaphor for troubled times and the assurance that God would liberate them. Others believed that resurrection was far off in the future. They wanted something more concrete, more immediate, more practical—something for the here and now.

Other religions were offering some kind of promise—most of them more practical, more joyful, and more pleasant (one of them promoted sexual rites among its religious practices). After all, many people believed that religion was supposed to provide hope to its followers and that a religion's success could be judged by its ability to produce dreams. In Corinth, religions were fighting for space and searching for believers. Each religion was selling dreams and offering better ways to live on earth.

Paul spends a large portion of this chapter talking about the uniqueness of the Christian promise of resurrection, the promise that everything will be completed and perfected in the future. Our hope for this is based on the person of Jesus Christ (vv. 1-4). He died for our sins, was buried as any other human being, but he was raised to life again. If he was resurrected, we can believe his promise to do the same with us. We can believe it because we have seen it happen in Jesus Christ. If we don't believe that he was resurrected, that he fulfills and completes the will of God, then we believe in vain (vv. 14, 17, 32).

> **We cannot finish Christ's mission. We work toward it, but the fulfillment of it lies a little beyond our grasp, urging us along.**

Jesus' resurrection came at the culmination of his ministry. It was a ministry that was finished, a mission accomplished with the delivery of the good news, yet it was a ministry not yet fulfilled. It was resurrected in the followers of Christ who were to carry on the ministry after Jesus left the earth. Thousands responded and the mission spread around the world. We cannot finish Christ's mission, however. We work toward it, but the fulfillment of it lies a little beyond our grasp, urging us along.

Now and Later

Resurrection is a real need for human beings. Other religions offer hope for fulfillment of their dreams in this life: money, success, a good family life, recognition, and power. But the human question remains: What is beyond death? Christianity replies that beyond death is the perfection of life that we all hope for. Jesus' death and resurrection are the signs that God's will will be fulfilled.

In many ways we see the resurrected Jesus in our midst. More than seventy refugees stowed away on a ship coming to the United States in order to escape political oppression in their homeland, but immigration officials got wind of the illegal aliens before they ever disembarked and arrested them in the port. The women were sent off to prison down south and the men were incarcerated in Pennsylvania as they awaited deportation hearings. A Christian man near one of the prisons heard of these refugees and went to visit them. He listened to their fears about returning to the repressive regime in their homeland, and their desire to live in a "free" land. He and his pastor mobilized their congregation to pray for and visit the prisoners, find legal counsel, teach them English, locate their families, educate themselves about the culture, and write letters to the attorney general and the president. After a visit with the refugees, a man from the congregation said he felt he had seen Jesus that day sitting across from him at the prison.

We know and feel that the resurrected Jesus is among us. But how will we be resurrected? How will God use us to fulfill the divine will? Paul explains something about this process in 1 Corinthians. He talks about the nature of the resurrection, saying that there will be a transformation from corruption to incorruption (v. 42), weakness to power (v. 43), and natural body to spiritual body (v. 44).

Promise Fulfilled

Resurrection is like a plant. "It is sown in dishonor, it is raised in glory" (v. 43*a*). Our life on earth is like a seed. It promises to be a glorious flower, but all we can see presently is an ordinary seed. The seed is the precursor to the flower; the seed promises to be fulfilled as a bloom. In this way life and the resurrected life are related.

Like the seed that carries the genetic material for the flower, we are to try to approximate the future that we know awaits. It is no good to say that I will be perfect then so I can behave any way I like in this life. Just as the seed cannot hope to be a butterfly in the future, we cannot hope to make perfection out of sin.

Our hope for the future determines how we will be now. Many people do not understand that Christ's resurrection among us means that we must carry on his mission, and the mission is to approximate the kingdom in anticipation of its coming in all its fullness later. If we believe in honesty, why would we promote corruption? If we believe in unity and love, why would we promote division here and now? We will never get to honesty and truth from corruption, nor unity from division.

Revolutionary Dreams

Hope is for tomorrow. If one doesn't dream, one doesn't live. Hope is the power that pushes us to live today looking at tomorrow. To dream is revolutionary; the one who dreams looks for tomorrow, not for today.

When Christians are looking forward, they are saying that they are not satisfied with this situation, with this "status quo." When Christians are satisfied with the injustices and hatreds in the present because they believe that the future will be full of justice, peace, sanctification, and honesty, they are fooling themselves. People for whom nothing has to be changed do not have dreams. Their satisfaction is here and now. They do not look forward with hope to the resurrection.

Faithful Christians have a commitment to justice, peace, love, sanctification, and the incorruptible life. It is not real in our present world, but our hope for a better future must move us today to act according to our hope. Oscar Romero planted the

> **When Christians are satisfied with the injustices and hatreds in the present because they believe that the future will be full of justice, peace, sanctification, and honesty, they are fooling themselves.**

seeds of hope in the people of El Salvador. The way has not been easy for them, but years after his death, they are still persevering toward the vision, living today out of their hope.

Our commitment is with Jesus Christ and his kingdom. We have a commitment to change, transformation, and renewal. We need to sing every day a new song, as the psalmist requests. We are pilgrims constantly walking to the promised land. God bless us in this journey!

Discuss and Act

1. Together summarize what 1 Corinthians 15 says. Return to the conversation started in "Share and Pray" about your understandings of life after death and eternal life. Let everyone speak freely; avoid debate or criticism of someone else's understanding. Talk about the importance of resurrection for your Christian belief.

2. The author says that we move toward fulfilling our hopes and dreams, which always lie a little beyond us, pulling us toward them. What are your dreams for the church? Do you have hopes that they will ever be fulfilled, even partially? Why?

3. Goodness cannot come from sin, nor unity from disunity. If we hope that the church will be unified in the end, we will have to work for unity now. As a group, create a plan to bring unity to your denomination, the wider Christian church, and the world. Dream!

4. What does it mean for the church to be the resurrected body of Christ until God's plan is fulfilled? Why is it better for the Corinthian church—and for ours—to be unified in this mission? Can individuals be effective in doing God's work alone? Why, or why not?

5. Recall the definition of sanctification from session 1. How does the sanctified life relate to resurrection?

6. Review the sessions in this study, inviting comments and reflections on highlights or remaining questions. Then ponder these questions: How has the study of 1 Corinthians changed the way you think about the church? How important was the church in your Christian beliefs before? How important is it now?

7. In prayer, name the themes of this study (community, diversity, unity, wisdom, gifts, love, hope, and resurrection), pausing between each to allow sentence prayers.

Resource Pages

Forming a Covenant Group

Covenant-making is an important part of the biblical story. God made covenants with the people, beginning with Noah and Abram. Many of the prophets spoke of broken covenants and the need for renewing covenant; Jesus called people to new understandings of the covenant with God. He also called the early church to be in covenant with God and with each other.

As Christians today, we also covenant with God and with each other. These covenant commitments help us live out our faith. As we come together in a small group to share, pray, study God's Word, and seek to live our faith, the Spirit's presence empowers us to live our covenants.

As a covenant group, you will make commitments with each other. Ask yourselves these questions to help you decide about the kinds of commitments that will guide your group life:

- What are our hopes, fears, expectations for this covenant group?
- What are our expectations about being present at all meetings? How will we handle unavoidable absences?
- How can we help each person participate fully in our sharing and prayer time? In our Bible study?
- How will we work together to build trust? How can we work at keeping confidences? What are the important areas of congregational life for each of us? How will we continue to participate fully in the congregation's life and work?

Whether you start with sharing and prayer or end with it, consider setting this special time apart by beginning each of the next ten weeks' sharing and prayer experiences in the same manner. This signals that this is a sensitive and sacred time to enter into God's presence together as a community, bound together by love and a common faith in God. Start each session by joining hands in a circle (either sitting or standing is fine) and taking three deep breaths. Spend one to two minutes in silence, preparing your hearts and minds for sharing and prayer. Make time for everyone to check in and share about where they are at that given moment.

Feel free to make up your own ritual and create a setting that fits your group. For ideas, you might begin each session with a hymn, use a candle or candles, begin or end with the same prayer each time, or create a small banner that illustrates the theme and have it present for each session.

A Covenant Prayer

O God, we renew the covenant,
spoken by our fathers and mothers,
> sung in homes and meetinghouses,
> written by the pens of pilgrims and preachers.

This covenant we know is costly;
> but there is nothing of greater value.

So we accept your gifts and promises,
> with thanksgiving;

And offer you our lives and our love. Amen.

By Leland Wilson. Adapted from *The Gifts We Bring*, Vol. 2. Church of the Brethren General Board, Elgin, Ill.

Resources for Communion

Lover of Our Bodies and Souls

Lover of Our Bodies and Souls,
in a world overwhelmed by division
You draw the fragmented parts
of ourselves into unity with You,
and enlighten us with the wholeness
      of our being.
Make us willing receivers
      of the Bread of Life:
that, filled with the knowledge
      of your loving kindness,
we embody the fullness
which you have given us in Christ;
Mother of All, Bread of Life,
Cup that Overflows. Amen.

Reprinted from *Seasons of the Feminine Divine*, by Mary Kathleen Speegle Schmitt. Copyright © 1993 Crossroad. Used by permission.

Communion

Gently—like rain on a spring-warm day—
      the words fell
           into my face,
    splashing, rolling, embedding
        in the burrows of my being:
THE BLESSINGS OF CHRIST BE WITH YOU.
There in the midst of broken bread
      in a world of broken bodies
           and splintered spirits
the communion of saints
      became new again,
washed once more
      in blessing and promise.

Reprinted from *Searching for Shalom: Resources for Creative Worship* by Ann Weems. Copyright © 1991 Ann Barr Weems. Used by permission of Westminster/John Knox Press.

Gift of God

Gift of God
You
        sit next to me and
                pass me Bread and Wine . . .
You
        always there
                with communion in your countenance
        reaching ready
                aware accepting affirming

Gift of God
You
        touch this lepered me
                to wholeness

Instrument of God
You
        hear alleluias through obscenities
                see rainbows in the darkest storms
                        unearth flowers in the snow

Gift of God
I thank God for you!

Reprinted from *Reaching for Rainbows* by Ann Weems. Copyright © 1980 Ann Weems. Used by permission of Westminster/John Knox Press.

Resources for Praying Together
Our Gifts Are Gifts of Hope

Our yearning after God,
    our hope for a better way
        creates infinite possibilities
            to touch the lives of the untouched

            to reach the hearts
                of the unreached

            to heal the wounds
                of the unhealed

            to feed the bodies
                of the unfed

            to accept the personhood
                of the unaccepted

            to love the being
                of the unloved

Our gifts are gifts of hope;
O God,
    touch
        reach
            heal
                feed
                    accept
                        and love us

    that we might love one another.

Reprinted from *Searching for Shalom: Resources for Creative Worship* by Ann Weems. Copyright © 1991 Ann Barr Weems. Used by permission of Westminster/John Knox Press.

Faith, Hope, and Love

With faith and hope and love we come,
Intent upon our quest
To be, with Christ, more venturesome,
Pursuing what is best.

We would not be as noisy gongs
Or clanging cymbals bold,
For all of life to God belongs,
And God, with love, upholds.

Prophetic powers are not enough
And faith is incomplete,
If we use knowledge to rebuff
The people whom we meet.

True love is patient, kind, and true,
Rejoicing in the right.
It does not childish ways pursue,
Nor arrogance invite.

No jealousy or boastful talk
Will mar the coming days,
For love endures along life's walk,
Not rude, resentful ways.

Grant understanding, and forgive
All care that just pretends.
Perfect in us the will to live
In love that never ends. Amen.

Reprinted with permission from *Refreshing Rains of the Living Word* by Lavon Bayler. Copyright © 1988 The Pilgrim Press.

New Shoots

Born in the light of the Bright and Morning Star,
    we are new.
Not patched, not mended . . . but new
    like a newborn . . .
    like the morning . . .
The guilt-blotched yesterdays are gone;
    the soul stains are no more!
There is no looking back;
    there are no regrets.
In our newness, we are free.
In the power of God's continuing creation,
    we are:
    new shoots from the root of Jesse,
    new branches from the one true Vine,
    new songs breaking through the world's deafness.
This then is a new day.
New Shoots, new branches,
new songs, new day . . .
Bathed in the promise of God's New Creation,
    we begin!

From *Searching for Shalom* by Ann Weems. Copyright © 1991 Ann Barr Weems. Used by permission of Westminster/John Knox Press.

Bibliography

Barclay, William. *The Letter to the Corinthians.* Daily Study Bible Series. Westminster John Knox, 1975.

Finger, Reta Halteman and George McClain. *Creating a Scene in Corinth: A Simulation.* Herald Press, 2013.

Hays, Richard. *First Corinthians.* Interpretation: A Bible Commentary for Teaching and Preaching. Westminster John Knox, 1999 (paperback, 2011).

Sampley, J. Paul, Robert W. Wall, and N. T. Wright. *Acts—1 Corinthians.* The New Interpreter's Bible Commentary Series, vol. 10. Nashville: Abingdon, 2002.

Snyder, Graydon F. *First Corinthians: A Faith Community Commentary.* Mercer University Press, 1992.

Stevens, Paul, and Dan Williams. *Corinthians 1: The Challenge of Life Together.* LifeGuide Bible Studies. InterVarsity Press, 1988.

Talbert, Charles H. *Reading Corinthians.* New York: Crossroad Publishing Company, 1989.

Websites

www.biblegateway.com is a searchable online Bible in 150 version and 50 languages

www.textweek.com is a virtual study desk for students, teachers, and preachers with links to commentaries and other resources